MANSFIELD TO DONCASTER

via Shirebrook & Shireoaks

Vic Mitchell and Keith Smith

Middleton Press

Front cover: No. 170506 waits at Mansfield Woodhouse in 2004. The station had reopened to passengers on 20th November 1995. (J.C.Haydon/Colour-Rail.com)

Back cover: Railway Clearing House map of 1947.

Published October 2018

ISBN 978 1 910356 23 4

© Middleton Press, 2018

Production Editor & Cover Design Deborah Esher
Typesetting & Design Cassandra Morgan

Published by
    Middleton Press
    Easebourne Lane
    Midhurst
    West Sussex
    GU29 9AZ
Tel: 01730 813169
Email: info@middletonpress.co.uk
www.middletonpress.co.uk

Printed and bound by CPI Group (UK) Ltd, Croydon, CR0 4YY

CONTENTS

1. Mansfield to Doncaster	1-92
2. Sutton-in-Ashfield to Shirebrook North	93-120

INDEX

56	Anston	61	Maltby	54	Shireoaks
59	Dinnington & Laughton	1	Mansfield Town	97	Skegby for Stanton Hill
89	Doncaster	11	Mansfield Woodhouse	93	Sutton-in-Ashfield Town
34	Elmton & Creswell	106	Pleasley	76	Tickhill & Wadworth
28	Langwith	117	Shirebrook North	42	Whitwell
113	Langwith Junction	108	Shirebrook South		
32	Langwith-Whaley Thorns	19	Shirebrook West		

ACKNOWLEDGEMENTS

We are very grateful for the assistance received from many of those mentioned in the credits, also from A.J.Castledine, G.Croughton, G.Gartside, A.C.Hartless, J.Hinson (Signalling Record Society), C.M.Howard, N.Langridge, B.Lewis, D. and Dr S. Salter, T.Walsh and, in particular, our always supportive families.

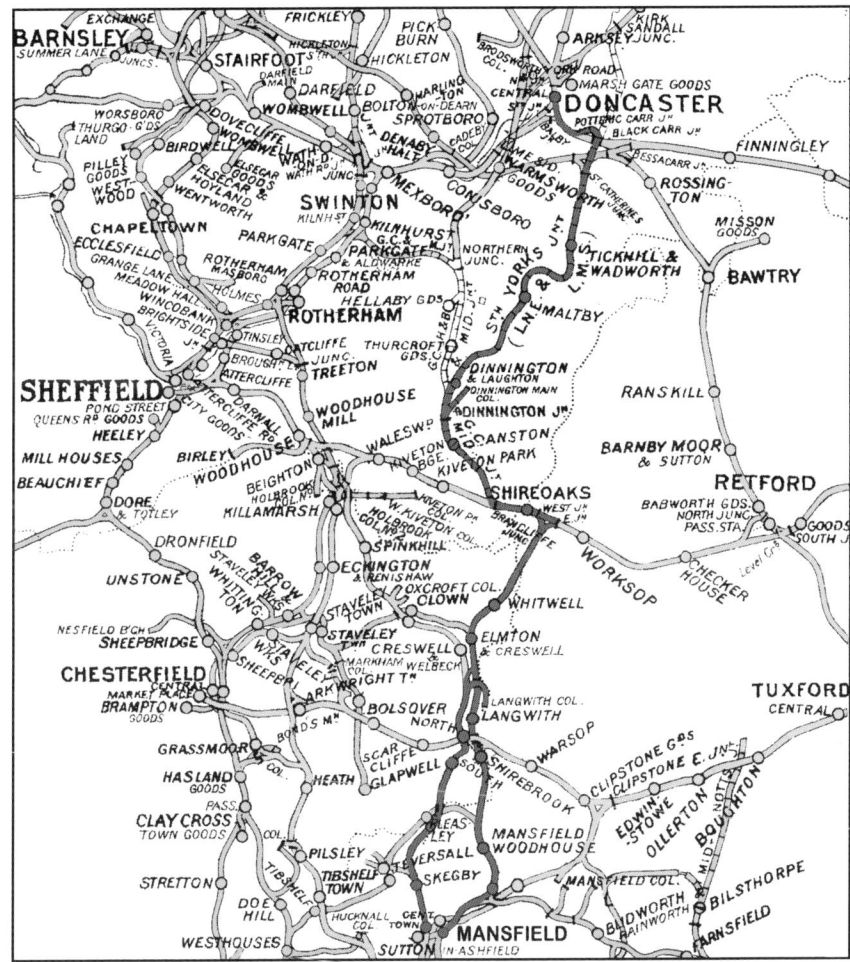

The 1947 Railway Clearing House map has the routes within this album shown with dark lines. It includes the connection near Creswell for the Robin Hood Line, which was added in 1993.

GEOGRAPHICAL SETTING

The journey in this album runs east of the Pennines and on the coalfields scattered on its foothills. Most of the route was constructed above limestone and red sandstones and passed over east-flowing rivers. From south to north they were the upper reaches of the Maun, the Meden, the Poulter, the Ryton and some brooks. A bridge was built at Shireoaks over the Chesterfield Canal; the River Don and its canal were encountered at Doncaster.

The line started near the eastern boundary of Derbyshire and entered Yorkshire south of Doncaster. The maps are to the scale of 25ins to 1 mile, with north at the top, unless otherwise indicated.

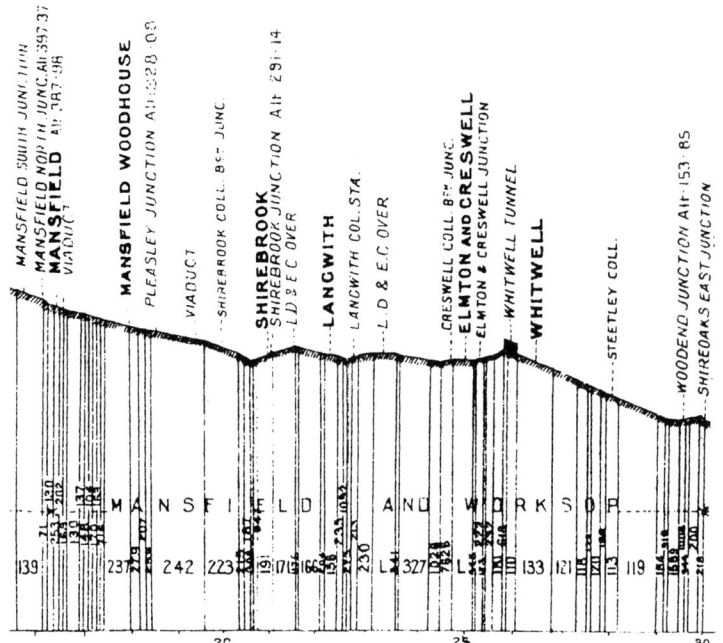

→ I. The 1946 map at ¼ ins to 1 mile has Mansfield lower centre and our route running northwards to Doncaster, which is top centre. Below it is Tickhill; its two nearest stations are shown with open circles, as they were closed. They were on our route. The high ground is shaded and the part south of Worksop is covered by Sherwood Forest, a name associated with Robin Hood.

HISTORICAL BACKGROUND

The Mansfield & Pinxton Railway (M&P) linked coal mines at both those places with the Cromford Canal at Pye Bridge as early as 1819. Wagons were horse drawn until 1848, and passengers were conveyed after 1832. On 9th October 1848 the Midland Railway opened its line from Nottingham to Kirkby where it met the M&P.

On 1st June 1875 the Midland extended northwards from Mansfield to Shireoaks and Worksop, meeting the Manchester, Sheffield & Lincolnshire Rly (later the Great Central) at both points. Passenger trains ran from Nottingham to Worksop until 12th October 1964, after which the line was freight only until passenger traffic was restored in the 1990s as the Robin Hood Line, described below.

The first railway to reach Doncaster was facilitated by the Lancashire & Yorkshire Rly's line from Knottingley in 1848. This made an end on junction with the infant Great Northern Rly at Shaftholme, four miles north of Doncaster. The GNR extended southwards from Doncaster to Retford in 1849 en route to London Kings Cross.

Lower right on map I is Blidworth, which saw MR passenger trains to Mansfield from Newark between 1871 and 1929. Mineral trains continued until 1965.

Opening late was the GNR line through Sutton-in-Ashfield, north to Shirebrook. It was built in 1898-1901 via Skegby, but passenger use of the three stations ended in 1931. The route closed to freight in 1968.

The route north from Shireoaks was operated by a Great Central & Midland Committee and was opened to the Anston area for freight in 1905. The two lines north thereof came into use in 1909, the

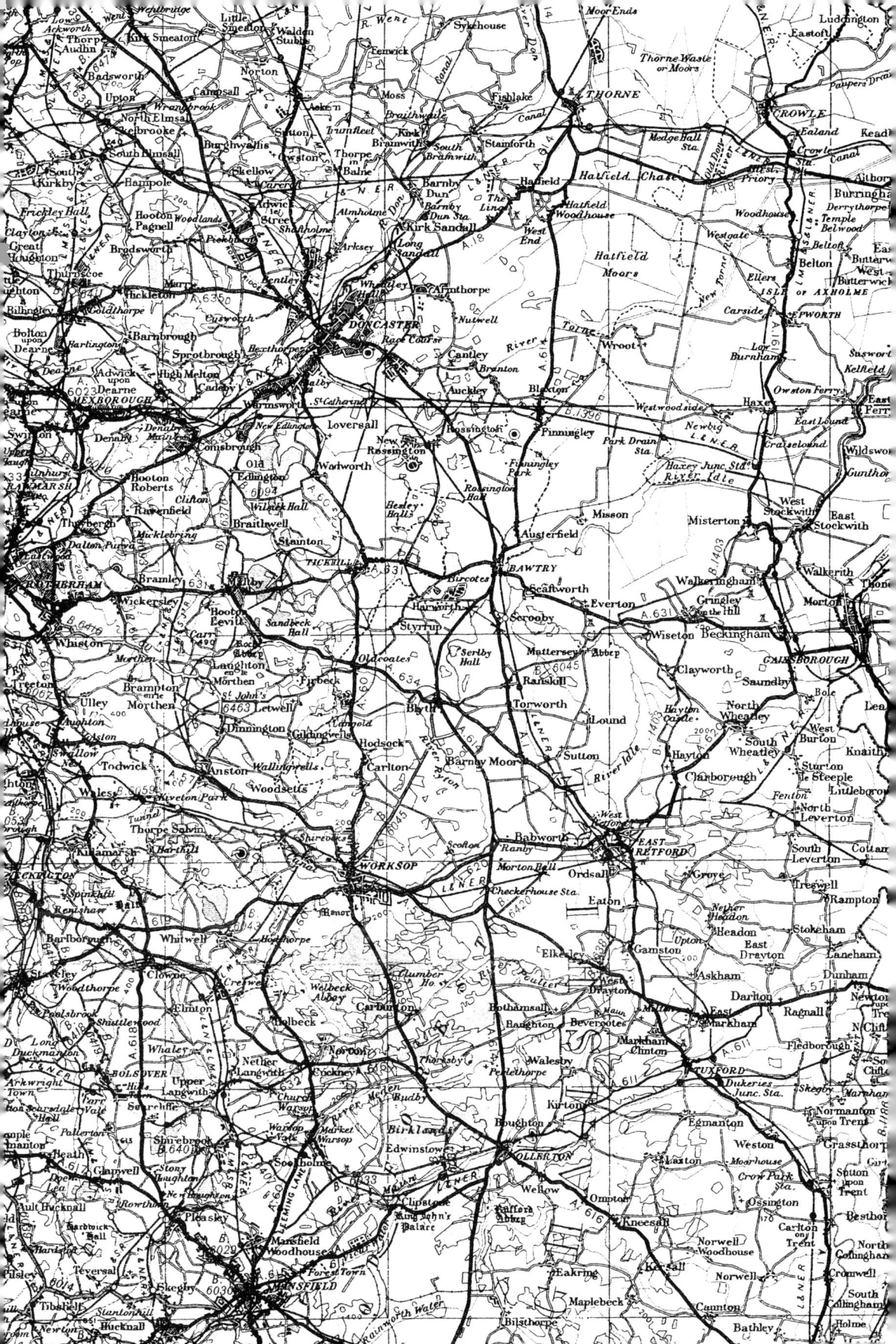

eastern one passing over the GNR main line and having a direct connection with it to Doncaster. The route ended two miles northeast of that town on the 1866 line to Goole; its northern section having been the South Yorkshire Joint Line. There was a passenger service between Shireoaks and Doncaster from 1st December 1910 until 2nd December 1929, with one gap in 1926-27. See captions 80-81 for more details.

The Manchester, Sheffield & Lincolnshire Railway opened most of its route between those places in 1849 and it is shown across the centre of map I. It became the Great Central Railway in 1897.

The Lancashire, Derbyshire & East Coast Rly (LDECR) opened in 1896 from Langwith Junction (later Shirebrook North) eastwards to Lincoln, and in 1897 westwards to Chesterfield. It was launched as a competitor to the Great Central, but ran out of money without reaching either Lancashire or the East Coast. Ironically it was taken over by the GCR in 1907.

The Mansfield Railway was built northeast from Mansfield in 1911-16 for mineral traffic. It was acquired by the GCR and passengers were carried from 2nd April 1917 until 2nd January 1956. Some holiday traffic lasted until 1964.

The Grouping of 1923 resulted in the GNR, the GCR and the GER becoming part of the London & North Eastern Railway. The MR formed part of the London Midland & Scottish Railway.

Nationalisation in 1948 brought much of the LNER into the Eastern Region of British Railways and the LMSR mainly into its London Midland Region. Subsequent branch closures are noted in the captions.

The first stage of the Robin Hood Line was initially operated by the Regional Railways Central division of BR. Upon privatisation, this became Central Trains, operated by National Express. This franchise commenced in March 1997 and saw the opening of the final stage of the Robin Hood Line in 1998. The franchise saw its boundaries amended and a new East Midlands Trains franchise, operated by Stagecoach, took over in November 2007. This was scheduled to operate until August 2019. In 2004, the route between Bulwell and Hucknall was reduced to single track. This enabled Nottingham Express Transit trams to operate alongside the route in this area.

The Robin Hood Line reopened as follows: Nottingham to Newstead on 17th May 1993 and on to Mansfield Woodhouse on 20th November 1995. New stations were provided at Sutton Parkway and Mansfield Woodhouse. Kirkby-in-Ashfield was opened on 18th November 1996. Finally, the Mansfield Woodhouse-Worksop section reopened on 25th May 1998, with stations at Shirebrook, Langwith-Whaley Thorns, Creswell and Whitwell. The construction was undertaken by Railtrack.

PASSENGER SERVICES

Via Mansfield Woodhouse

Destinations of northbound trains from Mansfield have varied over the decades. They have included Chesterfield, Sheffield, Retford and Doncaster. After many years of change, Worksop became the most common terminal point.

Trains numbered three in 1876 and 1894. There were up to six in the 1911 and 1947 timetables. They numbered up to nine in the final one in 1964. There were often extras on Saturdays in the later years. Upon reopening in 1998, a basic hourly service was provided, but again weekdays only and terminating at Worksop. By 2000, there were 18 trains (26 on Saturdays). Sunday trains began in May 2011.

Shireoaks to Doncaster

The initial service began in 1911 with three weekday trains. No evidence of Sunday trains has been seen. The number was down to two by 1928, the service operating from Worksop. In the months prior to closure in 1929, the sole train did not run north of Maltby, for passengers, apparently working empty from and back to Doncaster.

Skegby Route

By 1899, there were seven trains between Skegby, Sutton-in-Ashfield and Nottingham, on weekdays only. Two served Sutton on Sundays. This GNR service was extended north to Shirebrook in 1911 and, by 1914, there were eight weekday trains running over the entire route, with two on Sundays, all starting at Nottingham. The last through trains were in 1930, when there were six terminating at Shirebrook North, plus three more on Saturdays, but none on Sundays.

SHEFFIELD. SHIREOAKS, & MANSFIELD.—M.S.&L.

Mls	Victoria Sta.,	mrn	aft	aft	Mls		mrn	aft	1&3
—	**Sheffield** ..dep	8 55	1 55	6 35	—	**Mansfield** dep	1035	3 10	8 10
2	Darnall......	9 1	2 0	6 41	1½	Mansfield W **b**	1039	3 14	8 15
5¼	Woodhouse J.	9 10	2 7	6 50	4½	Shirebrook **b**	1047	3 22	8 23
10¼	Kiveton Park	9 22	2 19	7 2	6	Langwith **b**..	1051	3 26	8 28
13¼	**Shireoaks** ..	9 30	2 26	7 10	8¾	Cresswell **b**..	1055	3 30	8 33
17¼	Whitwell **a**..	9 40	2 36	7 20	10	Whitwell **b**..	1059	3 34	8 38
18¾	Cresswell **a**..	9 45	2 40	7 25	14¼	Shireo'ks 228	11 8	3 43	3 48
21½	Langwith **a**..	9 52	2 46	7 32	17¼	Kiveton Park	1116	3 51	8 56
23	Shirebrook **a**	9 57	2 50	7 37	22¼	Woodhouse J.	1127	4 2	9 7
26	Mansfield W **a**	10 5	2 57	7 45	25½	Darnall	1135	4 8	9 15
27½	**Mansfield** 195	1010	3 0	7 50	27¼	Sheffield 230a	1145	4 15	9 25

a Stop to set down only. **b** Stop to take up only.

June 1876

MANSFIELD, WORKSOP, and RETFORD.—Midland.

Mls		c	mrn	c	c	aft		Mls	*From Hull, page 447.*	c	aft	c	c	aft
—	**Mansfield** ....dep.	7 0	1150	Weds only.	4 20	6 24	....	—	**Retford**..........dep.	8 23	1 0	3 42	4 48	....
1½	Mansfield Woodhouse.	7 4	1157		4 24	6 28	....	3¾	Checker House	8 31	**b**	....	4 56	....
4½	Shirebrook	7 11	12 4		4 31	6 35	....	7¾	**Worksop** ...... arr.	8 40	1 12	3 53	5 7	....
									dep.	8 50	1 13	4 15	5 15	7 14
6	Langwith	7 15	12 9		4 35	6 39	....	12½	Whitwell	9 1	1 23	4 26	5 25	7 24
8½	Elmton and Creswell..	7 20	1215	2 47	4 40	6 45	....	14	Elmton and Creswell..	9 6	1 27	4 32	5 28	7 27
10½	Whitwell	7 26	1220	3 52	4 47	6 49	....	16¾	Langwith	9 14	1 33	Weds only.	5 35	7 35
15	**Worksop 447, 443** arr.	7 35	1230	3 3	4 58	6 58	....	18¾	Shirebrook	9 18	1 37		5 40	7 40
	dep.	7 49	1233	4 16	6 16	....	....	21¼	Mansfield Woodhouse.	9 24	1 43		5 46	7 46
19	Checker House	7 57	**a**	4 24	6 24	....	....	22¾	**Mnsfield 367, 368, 369**	9 30	1 47		5 52	7 52
22¾	**Retford 444**......arr..	8 5	1247	4 32	6 32	....	....							

a Stops when required to set down from Whitwell and other Midland Stations. **b** Stops when required to take up for Whitwell and beyond. **c** Change at Worksop.

November 1894

Table 236 NOTTINGHAM, SUTTON JUNCTION, MANSFIELD, and WORKSOP

Miles		Week Days																	Sundays				
		a.m	a.m		a.m	a.m	a.m S		p.m S	a.m		p.m	p.m	p.m	p.m	p.m	p.m		a.m ③	a.m ③		p.m ③	p.m ③
	208 London (St. Pan.) dep	9N10	..	..	..	4 15	8 55	..	..	1145	..	1255	..	3 15	..	4 50	6 40	..	12s0	10 0	..	2 50	4 55
	Nottingham........ dep	5 47	7 30	..	8 25	9 45	1211	..	..	3 7	..	4 33	5 12	6 4	6 35	7 40	1010	..	1010	1 25	..	7 0	9 10
2¼	Radford	5 53	7 36	..	8 31	..	1217	..	..	3 13	..	..	5 19	6 11	6 41	7 46	..	..	..	..	..	..	..
4	Basford	5 58	7 41	..	8 36	..	1222	..	..	3 19	..	4 42	5 24	6 16	6 46	7 51	1019	..	..	..	..	..	9 19
5½	Bulwell	6 5	7 50	..	8 41	9 56	1227	..	..	3 23	..	4 47	5 29	6 21	6 51	..	1024	..	1021	..	..	..	9 24
8½	**Hucknall**	6 15	7 58	..	8 49	10 4	1235	..	..	3 31	..	4 55	5 37	6 29	6 59	8 0	1032	..	1029	1 41	..	7 16	9 32
9¼	Linby	6 18	8 2	..	8 52	..	1239	..	..	3 35	..	4 58	5 41	6 32	7 3	8 5	1035	..	..	..	..	..	..
10½	Newstead	6 22	8 8	..	8 56	1011	1245	..	..	3 41	..	5 2	5 47	6 36	7 9	8 11	1039	..	..	1 47	..	..	9 38
11¼	Annesley	6 25	8 12	..	8 59	..	1249	..	..	3 45	..	5 5	5 51	6 39	7 13	..	1042	..	..	..	..	..	..
13¼	Kirkby-in-Ashfield	6 32	8 18	..	9 6	1019	1255	..	..	3 51	..	5 11	5 57	6 45	7 19	8 19	1048	..	1041	1 55	..	7 27	9 47
14¾	Sutton Junc. arr	6 35	8 21	..	9 9	1022	1258	..	..	3 54	..	5 14	6 0	6 48	7 22	8 22	1052	..	1044	1 58	..	7 30	9 50
	dep	6 39	8 22	..	9 10	1023	1259	..	..	3 55	..	5 15	6 1	6 49	7 23	8 23	1054	..	1046	1 59	..	7 31	9 51
17	**Mansfield** arr	6 43	8 26	..	9 14	1027	1 3	..	..	3 59	..	5 19	6 5	6 53	7 27	8 27	1058	..	1050	2 3	..	7 35	9 55
	dep	6 49	..	..	..	1036	..	..	1 52	4 4	..	..	6 10	6 58	..	8 32	..	..	..	..	..	..	..
18¾	Mansfield Woodhouse	6 56	..	..	..	1040	..	..	1 56	4 8	..	..	6 14	7 2	..	8 36	..	..	..	..	..	..	..
21¼	Shirebrook	7 3	..	..	..	1046	..	..	2 2	4 14	..	..	6 20	7 8	..	8 42	..	..	..	..	..	..	..
23	Langwith	7 9	..	..	..	1051	..	..	2 7	4 19	..	..	6 25	7 13	..	8 47	..	..	..	..	..	..	..
25¾	Elmton & Creswell	7 16	..	..	..	1057	..	..	2 12	4 25	..	..	6 31	7 19	..	8 53	..	..	..	..	..	..	..
27¾	Whitwell	7 21	..	..	..	11 2	..	..	..	4 30	..	..	6 36	7 24	..	8 58	..	..	..	..	..	..	..
32	**Worksop** arr	7 30	..	..	..	1111	..	..	..	4 40	..	..	6 45	7 33	..	9 7	..	..	..	..	..	..	..

a a.m. E or E Except Saturdays. *s* Saturday night. N Night time. Dep. 11 50 p.m. on Sundays. U Arr. 5 20 a.m on Sundays. S or S Saturdays only. ③ Third class only.

December 1947

NOTTINGHAM AND WORKSOP

WEEKDAYS ONLY

Miles						A SO		B SO	SX		SO	SX	SO			SO		SX	SO	SX		SO		SX			SX	SO
		a.m.	a.m.			a.m.	a.m.	a.m.	a.m.		a.m.	a.m.	a.m.		a.m.	p.m.	p.m.	p.m.	p.m.	p.m.		p.m.	p.m.	p.m.	p.m.		p.m.	p.m.
0	**NOTTINGHAM Midland** ......dep.	.	5 47	.	.	.	7 25	8 38	8 40	.	9 8	9 45	10 35	.	11 46	12 25	.	3 11	3 20	4 40	.	4 40	5 11	5 14	6 7	.	9 25	10 25
2¼	Radford	...	5 52	...	...	6 33	7 30	...	...	...	9 13	9 50	10 40	...	...	12 30	...	3 16	3 25	4 45	...	4 45	5 17	Via Pye Bridge	6 12	...	...	...
5½	Bulwell Market	.	6 2	.	.	6 44	7 39	8 48	8 49	.	9 20	9 57	10 47	.	.	12 37	.	3 24	3 33	4 52	.	4 52	5 25		6 19	.	.	.
8½	Hucknall Byron	...	6 13	...	...	6 52	7 47	8 57	8 57	...	9 29	10 5	10 55	...	12 0	12 45	...	3 32	3 42	5 0	...	5 0	5 33		6 27	...	9 40	10 40
9½	Linby	.	.	.	.	.	7 51	.	9 0	.	.	.	10 58	.	.	.	.	3 35	3 45	5 4	.	5 4	5 36		6 30	.	9 44	10 44
10¾	Newstead	...	6 20	...	...	6 59	7 57	9 4	9 4	...	9 36	10 11	11 2	...	12 6	12 51	...	3 39	3 49	5 10	...	5 10	5 40		6 34	...	9 50	10 50
13¼	Kirkby-in-Ashfield East	.	6 29	.	.	7 8	8 6	9 14	9 12	.	9 45	10 19	11 11	.	12 14	12 59	.	3 47	3 57	5 19	.	5 19	5 48	6 20	6 42	.	9 59	10 59
14¾	Sutton Junction	.	6 33	.	.	7 12	8 10	9 19	9 16	.	9 50	10 23	11 15	.	12 18	1 3	.	3 51	4 1	5 23	.	5 23	5 52	6 24	6 46	.	10 3	11 3
17½	**MANSFIELD Town**.........arr.	...	6 38	...	...	7 17	8 15	9 24	9 21	...	9 55	10 28	11 20	...	12 23	1 8	...	3 56	4 6	5 28	...	5 28	5 57	6 29	6 51	...	10 8	11 8
	" " ....dep.	5 30	6 48	.	.	7 22	.	9 29	.	.	10 0	10 34	11 25	.	12 28	.	2 34	4 1	4 11	5 34	.	.	6 5	.	6 56	.	.	11 14
18¾	Mansfield Woodhouse	5 34	6 52	...	...	7 26	...	9 33	...	...	10 4	10 38	11 29	...	12 32	...	2 38	4 5	4 15	5 39	...	...	6 9	...	7 0	...	...	11 18
21¾	Shirebrook West	5 44	6 59	.	.	7 34	.	9 41	.	.	10 11	10 45	11 36	.	12 39	.	2 45	4 12	4 22	5 45	.	.	6 16	.	7 7	.	.	11 25
23	Langwith	5 49	7 4	...	...	...	...	...	...	...	10 15	10 49	11 40	...	12 43	...	2 50	4 16	4 26	5 50	...	...	6 20	...	7 11	...	...	11 30
25¾	Elmton & Creswell	5 55	7 10	.	.	.	.	.	.	.	10 21	10 55	11 46	.	12 49	.	2 56	4 22	4 32	5 56	.	.	6 26	.	7 17	.	.	11 36
27½	Whitwell	6 0	7 15	...	...	...	...	...	...	...	10 25	10 59	11 49	.	12 53	.	3 1	4 26	4 36	6 0	...	...	6 30	...	7 21	...	...	...
32	**WORKSOP** ....arr.	6 11	7C26	.	.	.	.	.	.	.	10 37	11 10	12 0	...	1 6	...	3 12	4 42	4 50	...	.	.	6 44	.	7 32	.	.	.

A—Through Carriages to Skegness arr. 10.36 a.m. and to Mablethorpe arr. 10.48 a.m.
B—Through Carriages to Scarborough Central arr. 1.22 p.m. Runs until 29th August.
C—On Saturdays arrives Worksop 7.31 a.m.
D—Through Carriages 12.41 p.m. from Skegness and 12.25 p.m. from Mablethorpe to Radford.
E—Through Carriages 2.20 p.m. from Scarborough Central. Commences 27th June.
F—Arrives 3 minutes earlier.
SO—Saturdays only.
SX—Saturdays excepted.

September 1964

II. The 1954 edition at 1ins to 1 mile has our first station shown in rectangular form lower right. We journey to the top border, and Section 2 of this album is from the lower border northwards. It was ex-GNR.

Passing under it north of Pleasley is the former MR branch to Tibshelf. It carried passengers until 1930 and freight to 1982. The ex-MR branch to Sutton in Ashfield is close to the lower border and is nearly ½ mile long. It was in use from 1892 to 1951.

1. Mansfield to Doncaster

MANSFIELD TOWN

1. The station is seen in its prime on a postcard. It was closed to passengers on 12th October 1964 having gained the suffix TOWN on 11th August 1952. The goods yard received the term on 1st July 1950; parcels were more likely to be misdirected, one presumes. (LOSA)

2. This fine southward panorama was recorded on 29th June 1963 and in the foreground is the crossing for parcel trolleys. The staff crossing is between the middle of the platforms; here they were allowed to carry small items across. (E.Wilmshurst)

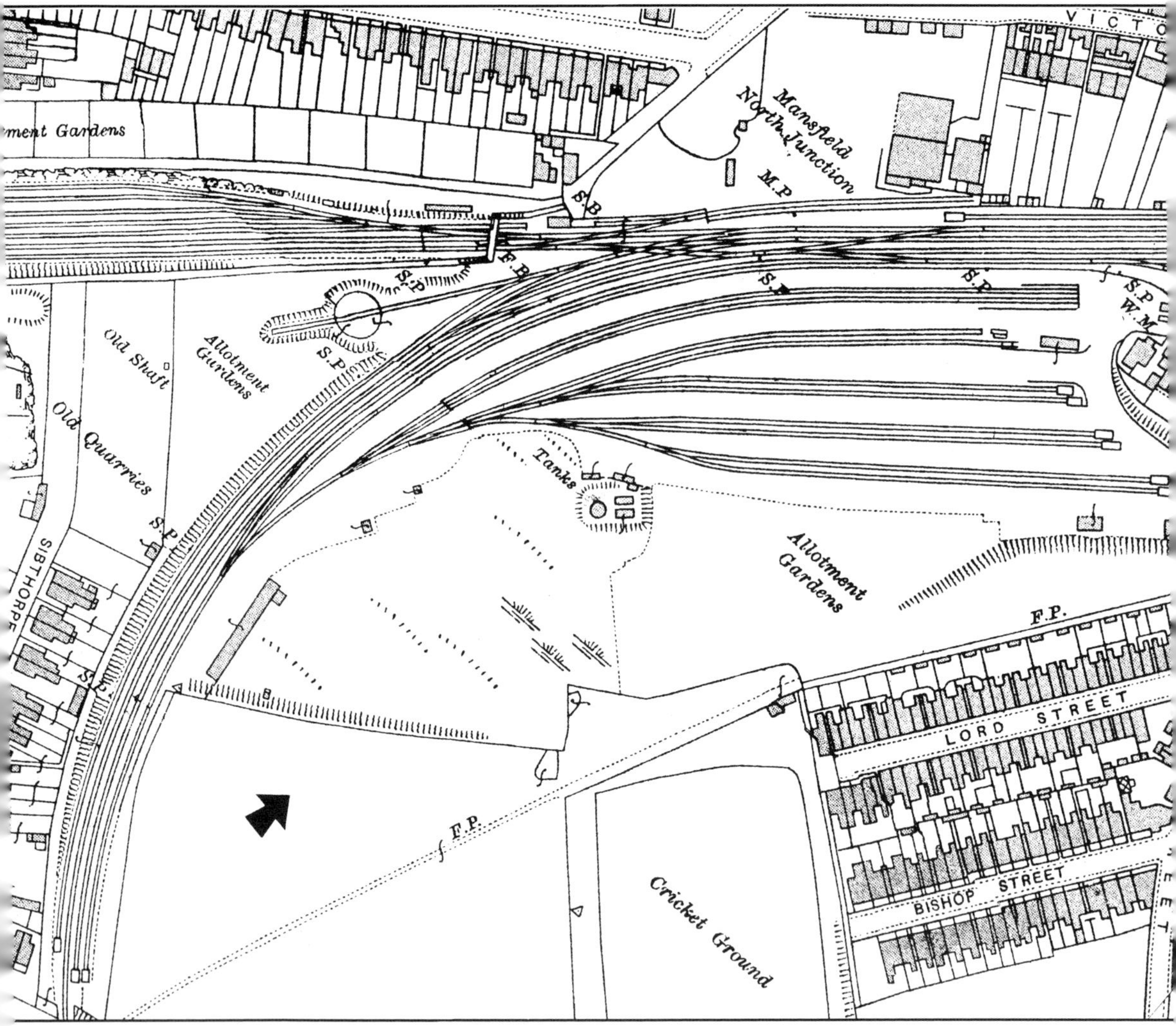

III. The street tramway is lower right and was that of Mansfield & District Light Railway Co Ltd. It was in use from 1899 until 1932. The 1917 survey has the route from Southwell lower left, from Nottingham top left, and our route on the right. The station was initially a terminus and it was south of the goods shed in 1849-72.

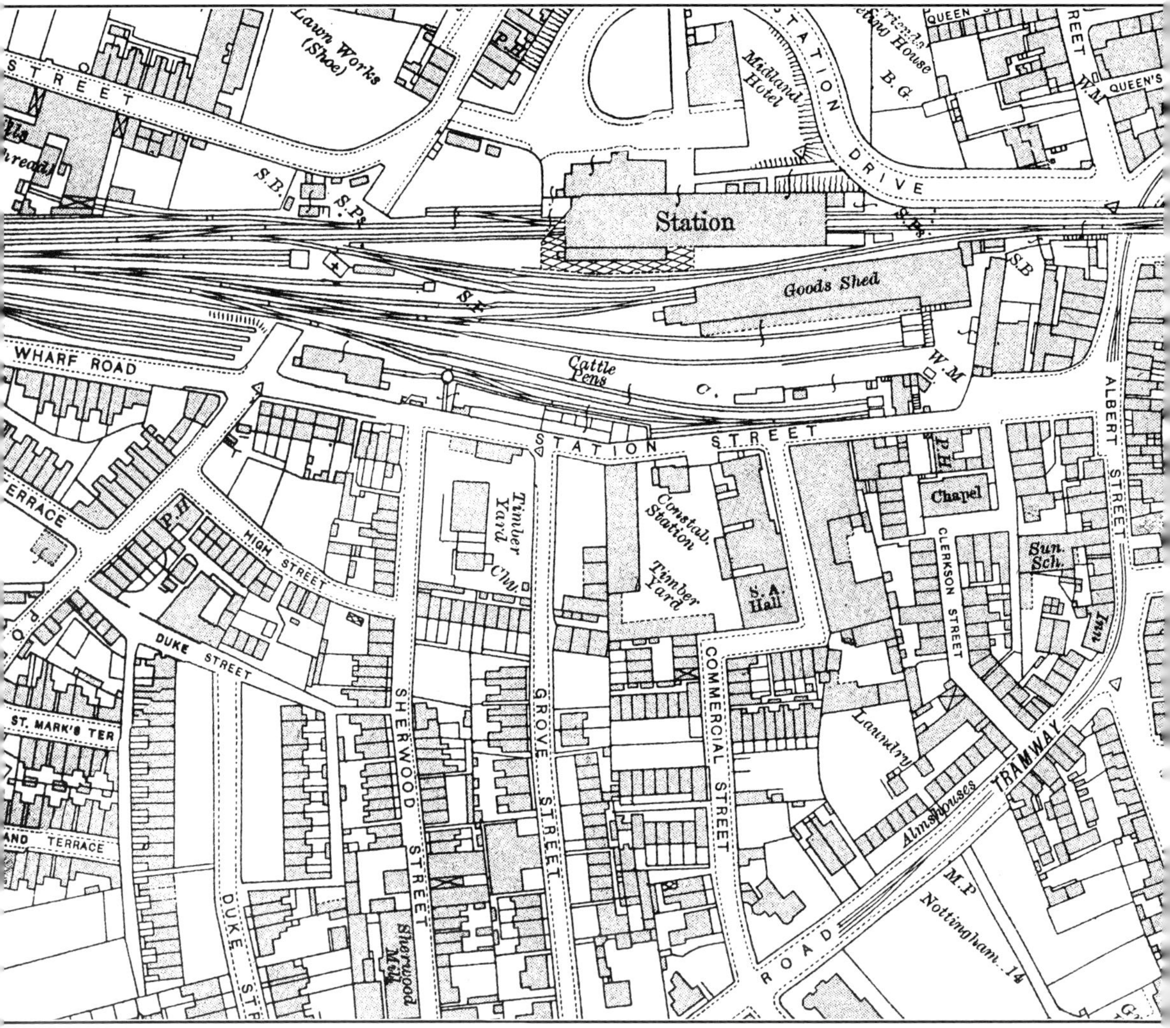

For other views of this station in the steam era see our *Nottingham to Lincoln* album; it includes the Southwell Branch.

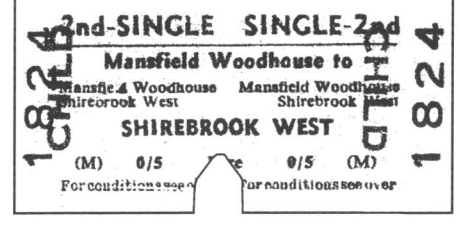
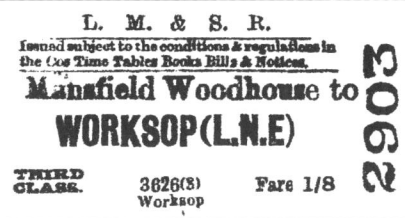

3. Seen on the same day is class 5 4-6-0 no. 45269 running in from Mablethorpe. The railings are around the stairwell and the subway roof is lower left, between the rails. (E.Wilmshurst)

4. Mansfield Station North Box is seen on the same day, as class 8F 2-8-0 no. 48413 runs past with an up coal train of great length. These signal arms rose up, not down. The box is MANSFIELD STATION NORTH. (E.Wilmshurst)

5. During the closure period, the town's claim to fame was that it was the largest in the UK devoid of a station. Restoration was recorded in progress on 18th February 1995. The suffix was dropped and it became Grade II listed. (R.J.Stewart-Smith)

6. The station buildings on Mansfield's down platform survived remarkably well given that the station was closed between 1964 and 1995. Single car no. 153365 calls with the 13.26 Nottingham to Worksop service on 1st September 2005. From 2012 to 2017, the annual passenger usage was recorded as 0.35 to 0.40 million. (P.D.Shannon)

NORTH OF MANSFIELD

Mansfield Viaduct

7. Just 10 chains long, the 12-arch structure starts close to the station and passes over several streets. Northbound in March 1956 is no. 44415, a class 4 0-6-0, a type introduced in 1924. (R.Humm coll.)

Sherwood Colliery

8. Sherwood Colliery Sidings South signal box is near the lower border of map IV, close to the Miners Rescue Station. It is seen on 19th September 1964. (R.Humm coll.)

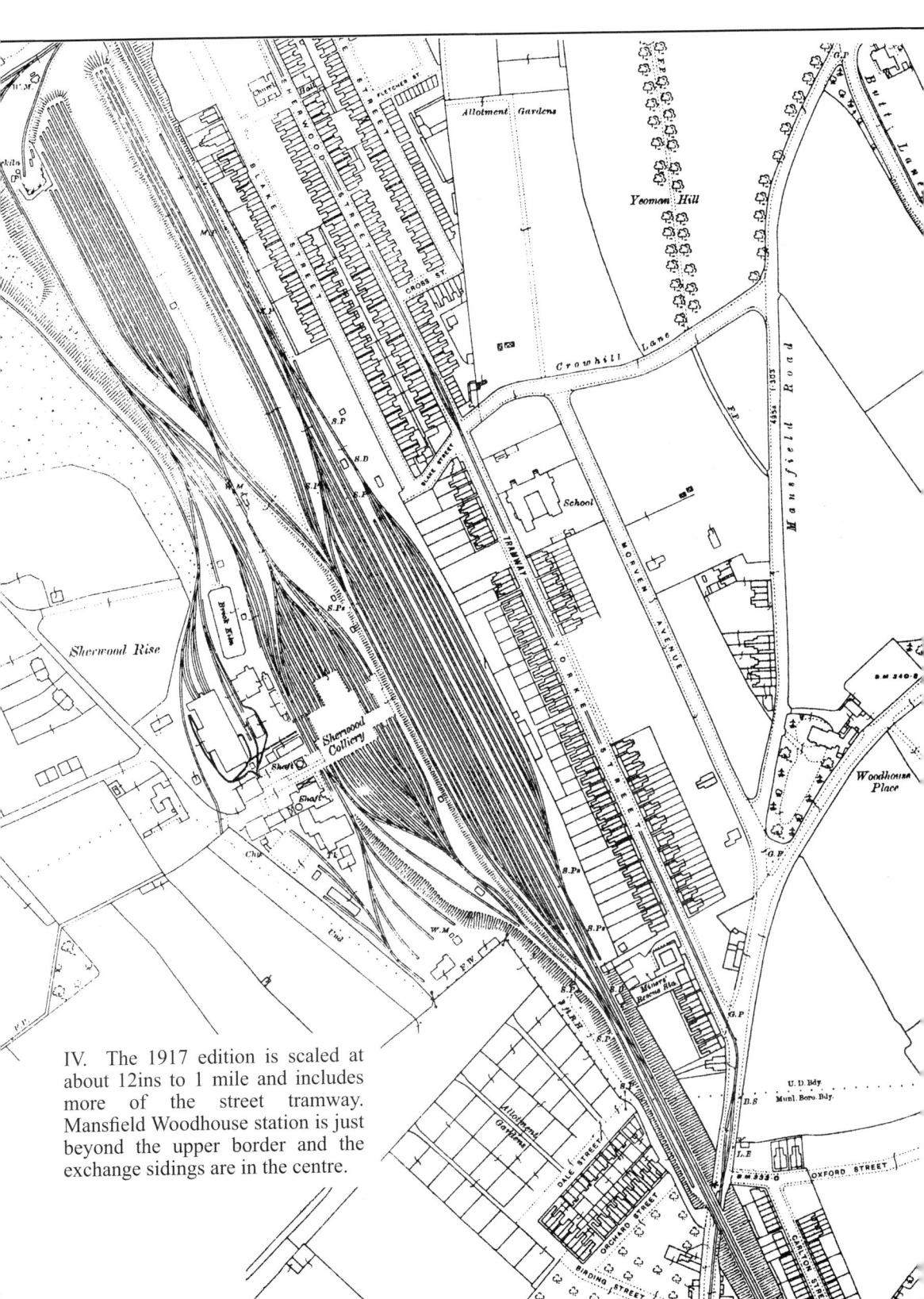

IV. The 1917 edition is scaled at about 12ins to 1 mile and includes more of the street tramway. Mansfield Woodhouse station is just beyond the upper border and the exchange sidings are in the centre.

9. We now see the taller North Box on 23rd September 1964 and the 3.47pm Worksop to Nottingham train, hauled by a 2-6-4T. Chimneys abound; most mine owners supplied coal free to their workers, simply tipping in the road by their front door. (R.Humm coll.)

10. No. 58048 creeps along the loading siding at Sherwood Colliery on 28th March 1991. Pit closure came in January 1992 and mining jobs in the area fell by almost 40,000 in 16 years. (R.J.Stewart-Smith)

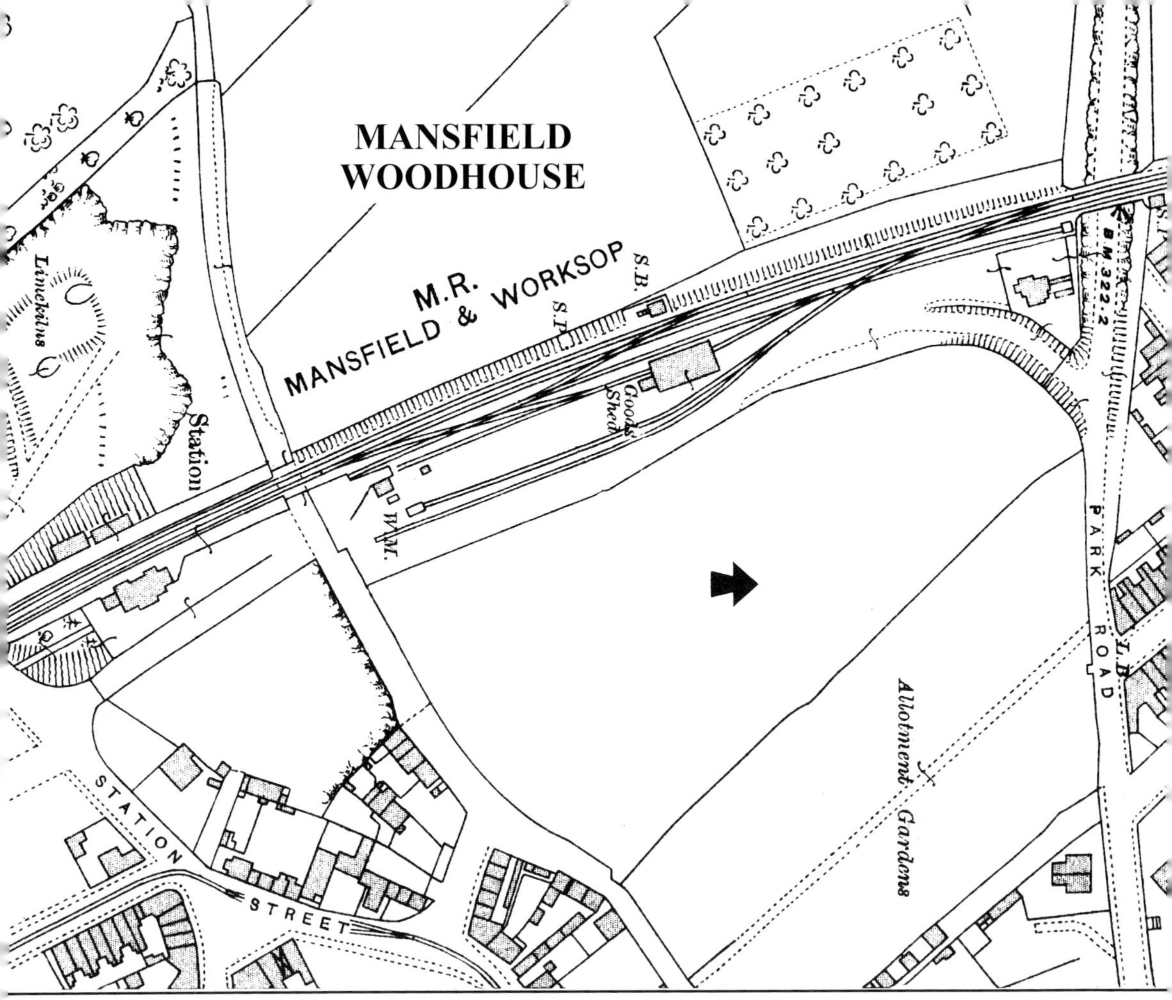

MANSFIELD WOODHOUSE

V. The station buildings and approach road are on the left of this 1916 extract. Part of the tramway is below them. Access to the goods yard is on the right, from Park Road.

11. This fine panorama from around 1900 is a view northwards and has the goods shed in the distance. The lamps are gas lit. The population was 21,445 in 1901, rising to 36,880 at the 1961 census. (J.Alsop coll.)

12. Little had changed by the time both signs for GENTLEMEN were recorded on 29th June 1963. The 4.0pm from Worksop to Nottingham was hauled by no. 42629, an ex-LMS class 4 2-6-4T. (E.Wilmshurst)

13. While passenger services ceased on 12th October 1964, freight continued until 2nd January 1967. The goods shed is seen on 1st May 1994, as work was progressing on the revival of the line. The small doorway indicates the location of the goods office. (R.J.Stewart-Smith)

14. No. 156412 calls on 17th April 2002 at around lunchtime. This is a service from Worksop to Nottingham formed of a class 156 unit in the then old Regional Railway livery with Central Trains branding. In the centre is the old goods shed, which was converted to a waiting shelter, when the Robin Hood line re-opened. (R.Geach)

15. Having been a temporary terminus for the Robin Hood Line since 1995, Mansfield Woodhouse became a through station again on 25th May 1998. Unit no. 158788 calls with the 10.40 Worksop to Nottingham train on 1st September 2005. The bay platform on the right ended in the old goods shed and was used for trains from Nottingham terminating here. Annual passenger use rose from around 155,000 in 2012 to almost 180,000 in 2017. (P.D.Shannon)

NORTH OF MANSFIELD WOODHOUSE

Pleasley Junction

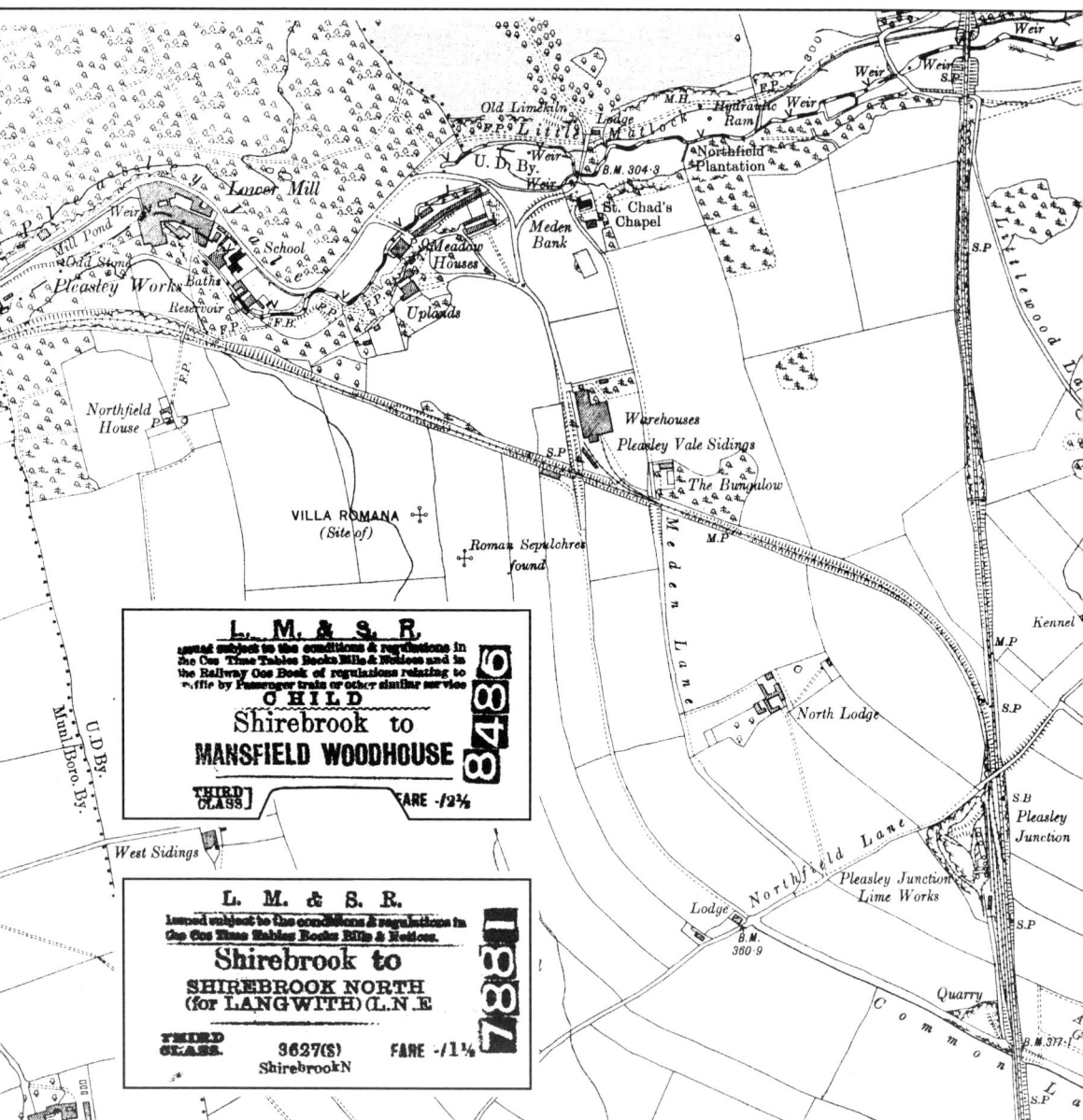

VI. The junction was about ½ mile north of Mansfield Woodhouse station and was opened by the MR to Pleasley in 1882. It was closed to Hollins Siding at Pleasley Vale warehouse (centre) in 1964 and to Pleasley in 1965.

SOUTH OF SHIREBROOK

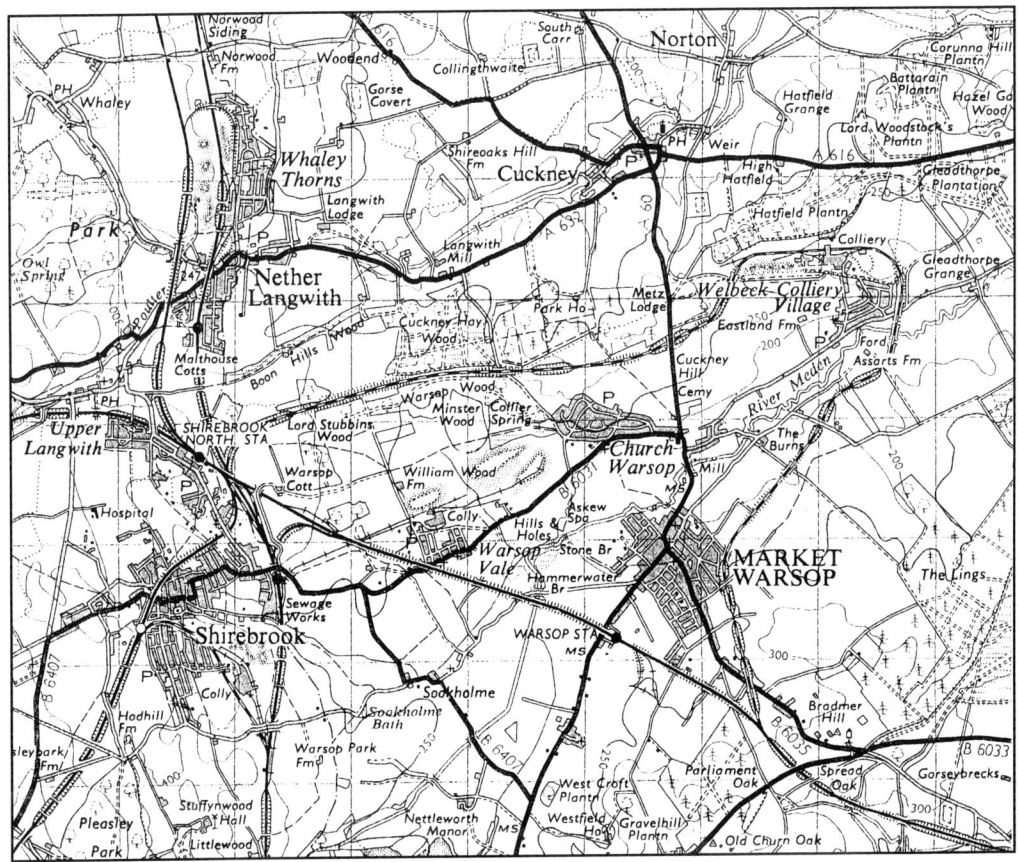

VII. The 1950 revision at 1ins to 1 mile has the ex-GNR line from Pleasley lower left and our route almost lower centre. The line branching left from it runs to Shirebrook South. Shirebrook West is above the 'S' of Sewage Works. Branching right is a mineral line to Warsop Colliery. This was productive from 1898 to 1989. Almost one mile to the north is one of two branches to Welbeck Colliery, which is mentioned in caption 33 in our *Chesterfield to Lincoln* album. It lasted from 1912 until 2011. Our journey continues to the top border; it is the right one of the two lines, at Norwood Siding. The next map shows more details of the area.

← VIII. Clearer at 6ins to 1 mile is the 1921 edition. It has the GCR diagonally top right. The MR is near the right border, with Shirebrook West station on it, unclear above the Gas Works. It is east of the town. The GNR's Shirebrook South station is west of its schools. Shirebrook Colliery is lower right and has branches from both railways. The MR line opened in 1875 and the GNR branch followed in 1901. A north-east curve linked the two lines from 1974. The station near the upper border was renamed Shirebrook North in 1924. The Gas Works had its own siding from its opening in 1902. By the mid-1930s, it was receiving around 6000 tons of coal per annum. Lower right was a halt for use by miners only. It was used from about July 1915 to July 1954. It was called Shirebrook Colliery Sidings from October 1945.

16. No. 56018 is at Shirebrook Colliery and is running round its set of empty MGR wagons on 29th March 1990. In Railfreight grey livery, it had just arrived with the empty wagons from Cottam Power Station (to the east of Retford) at 14.50 for loading under the rapid loader seen in the background. This site is now part of the Sports Direct warehouse complex, with all traces of the coal mine removed. No. 56018 was one of the first of 30 class 56 locomotives built in Romania during 1977. (R.Geach)

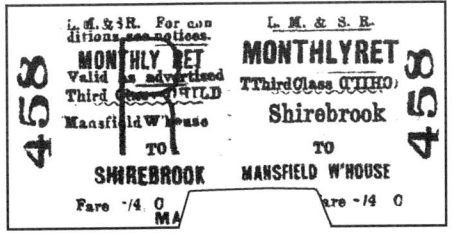

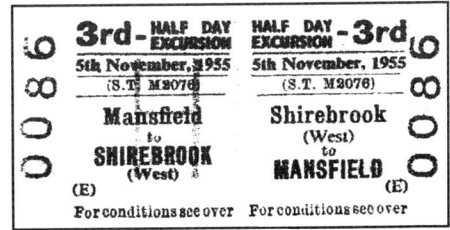

17. Work had begun in 1896 and two shafts were sunk, both 18ft in diameter. Coal was reached around 600yds down, but prolonged labour disputes and a typhoid outbreak delayed production seriously. The modernisation of loading arrangements was recorded on 26th August 1988. There was an underground link to Pleasley Colliery. (R.J.Stewart-Smith)

18. DMU no. T315 operated a special train for the Institute of Mining Engineers on 26th November 1989. Despite some sad records of gambling, alcoholism and a cage drop killing three miners, the mine was eventually a great success, exporting to most of Europe and also parts of Russia. Closure came in April 1993. (R.J.Stewart-Smith)

SHIREBROOK WEST

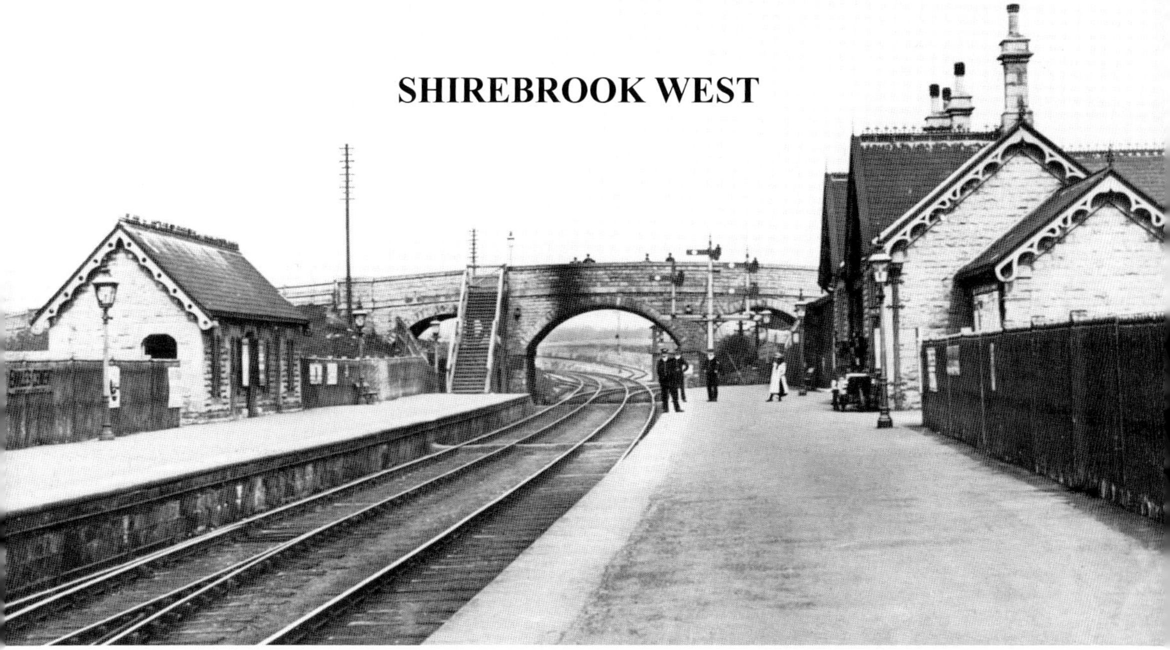

19. The population grew rapidly as coal mining expanded. The 1891 census showed 567 inhabitants, the figure growing to 6200 by 1901. This postcard from around that time shows that northbound passengers had to use the road bridge after purchasing their tickets. The suffix WEST was added on 18th June 1951. (P.Laming coll.)

20. The goods shed and the signal box are unclear in the distance in this view from the B6031 bridge on 25th June 1960. Working the 3.07pm Nottingham to Worksop is no. 40168, a class 3 2-6-2T of LMS origin. The station served passengers from 1st June 1875 until 12th October 1964. Its box closed on 17th January 1998. The curve from Warsop Colliery, plus its signals, are beyond the brake van. (R.Humm coll.)

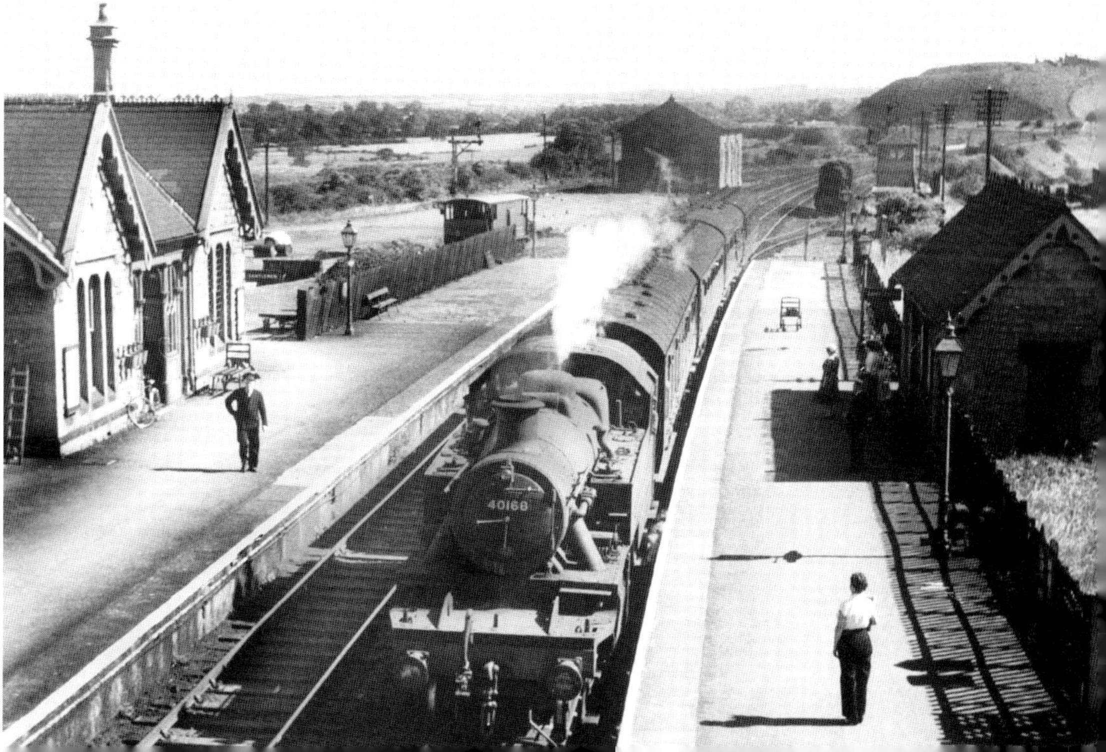

21. The goods yard closed on 1st May 1962 and its site received a diesel depot, which opened in 1965. It could serve 30 main line locos and 19 shunters. Initially, there were three tanks on tall towers outside the far end. These housed metallic grit, this having superseded sand as a traction aid. No. 56020 is seen on 26th July 1979, running towards the shed, which was coded 41J until 1973. It was then changed to SB. (T.Heavyside)

22. It is 25th October 1990 and the grit towers have long gone. Maintenance staff had initially numbered 70 and crew reached around 240, after Langwith shed closed (see captions 110-112). Part of the Warsop branch was relaid in 1976 for stabling purposes, but this ceased in 1991. A coach stands on it in this view. (R.J.Stewart-Smith)

23. Not obvious in the previous view is the all-important locomotive washing plant. Seen on the same day is no. 58038 and part of the Warsop Curve. Shed closure came on 28th September 1996 and demolition took place in July 2009. (R.J.Stewart-Smith)

24. This view is from almost the same camera position as picture 19. No. 156411 is running a Robin Hood Line service to Worksop on 21st March 2018. The station building had become the Shirebrook Business Centre in August 2017. (R.J.Stewart-Smith)

Shirebrook Junction

25. The curve between the MR and the LDECR opened in 1896, when the latter's main line here came into use. Taking the curve on 25th June 1960 is no. 48552, a class 8F 2-8-0. (R.Humm coll.)

26. The lineside vegetation had grown out of control by 26th July 1979. Southbound between duties are diesel shunters no. 08867 and 08560. They are returning to Shirebrook Shed. (T.Heavyside)

27. The 15mph sign and the almost level footpath for the signalman come into view. The empties from Cottam Power Station to Sherwood Colliery return behind no. 58016 on 4th April 1990.
(R.J.Stewart-Smith)

LANGWITH

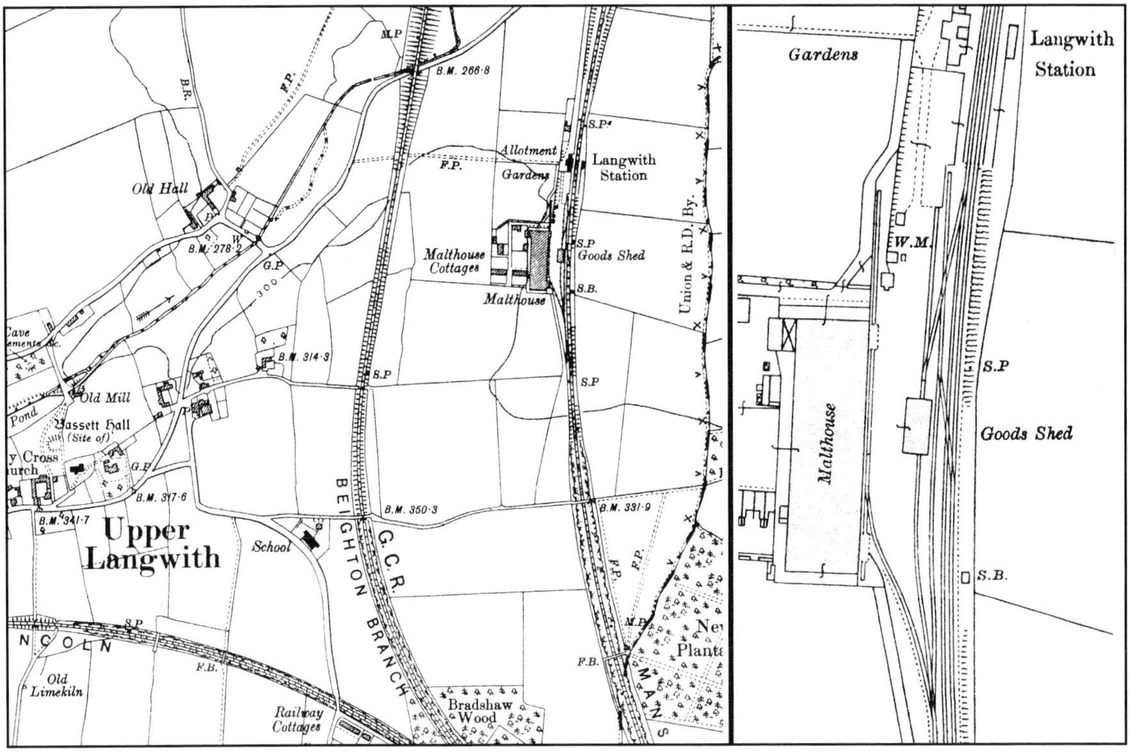

IX. Both maps are 1918 issues and are at 6 and 25ins to 1 mile. Our route is on the right of the former and the GCR to Lincoln is on its left. 'Langwith' is just an area and each community has a prefix. Lime was produced from a narrow stratum, which runs from north to south for miles. A kiln is lower left.

28. The station opened with the line and this early southward view includes the massive malthouse, centre. The hiding of sleepers with ballast soon became illegal. (R.Humm coll.)

29. Looking north, but at a later date, we see the massive chimneys of Langwith Colliery. The station's chimney pots vary in ornamentation. Unusually for an early picture, only one person faces the camera. (J.Alsop coll.)

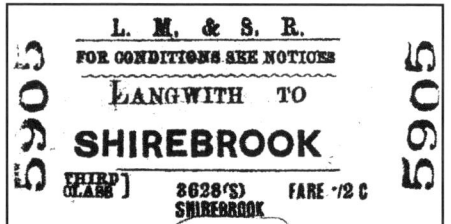 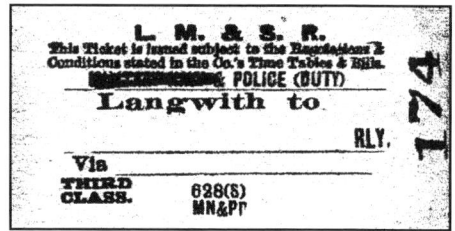

30. Seen on 18th August 1960 is the Saturdays only 10.50am Blackpool North to Radford service. It was used mainly by holidaymakers. It is hauled by class 5 4-6-0 no. 45270. Although overgrown, the goods yard did not close until 6th January 1964. The signal box was in use from 1897 to 1981. (R.Humm coll.)

31. All signage had vanished by the time of this view south, taken on 2nd May 1975. Passenger service on the route was withdrawn on 12th October 1964. It was delayed one week to serve the Nottingham Goose Fair. Demolition took place in 1978. (N.D.Mundy/J.Alsop coll.)

LANGWITH-WHALEY THORNS

32. The Robin Hood Line is shown on 13th April 1998. A new station was built ½ mile north of the original one. It opened on 25th May 1998; hence the lack of litter. Annual passenger figures grew from aournd 71,000 in 2012 to 87,000 in 2015. Most of the structures were painted light green and yellow. (R.J.Stewart-Smith)

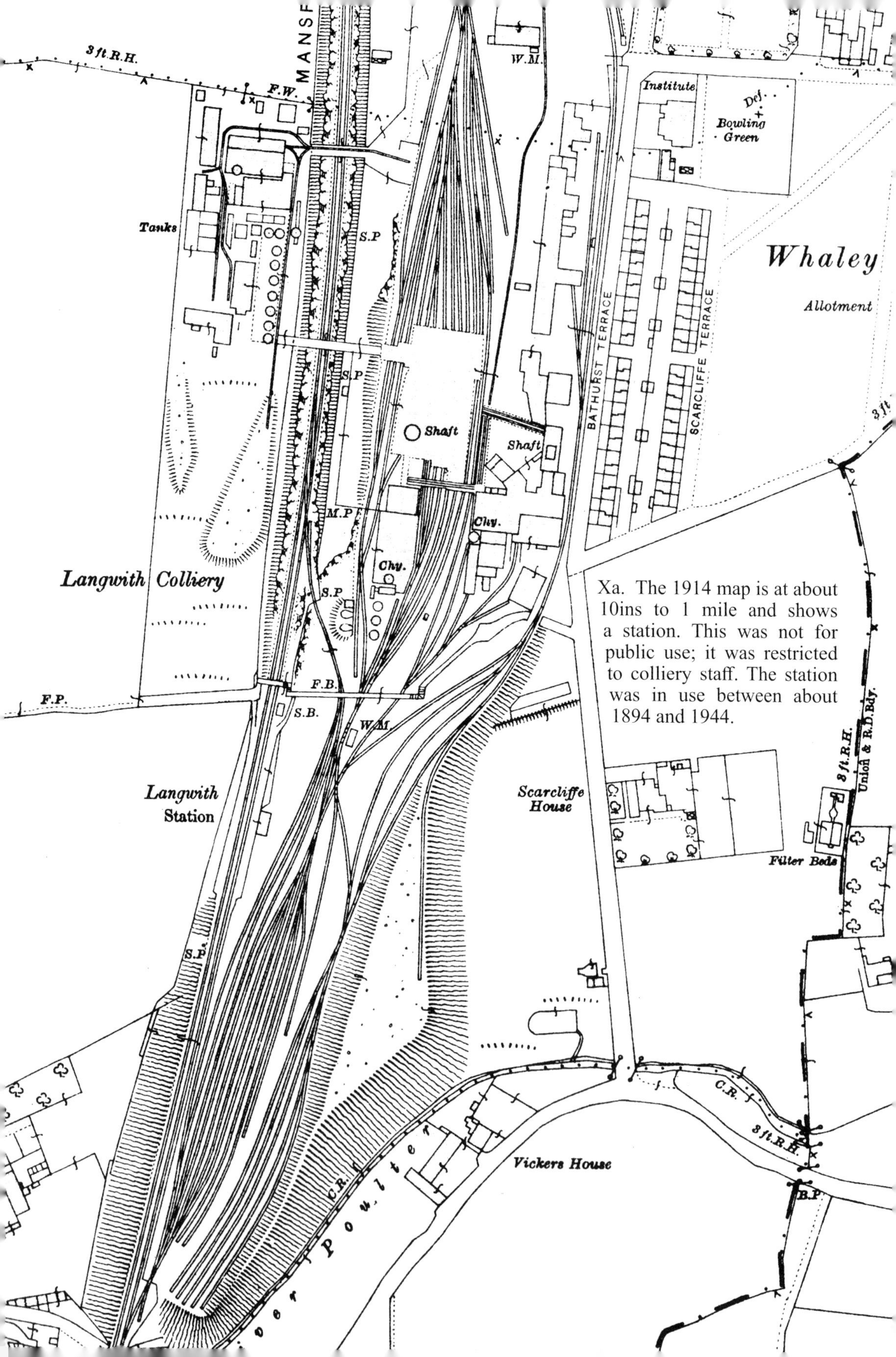

Xa. The 1914 map is at about 10ins to 1 mile and shows a station. This was not for public use; it was restricted to colliery staff. The station was in use between about 1894 and 1944.

NORTH OF LANGWITH

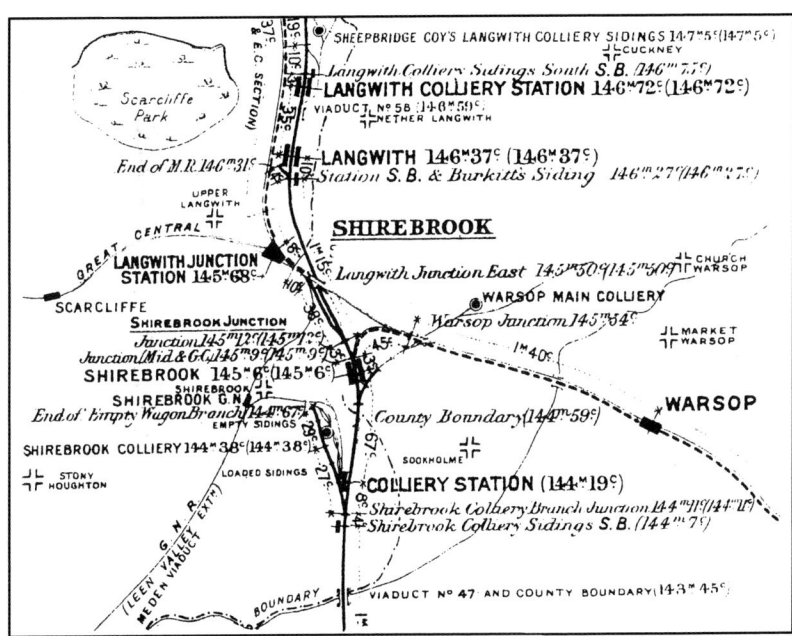

Xb. This MR diagram was dated 1912 and has the GCR across it. This is illustrated in our *Chesterfield to Lincoln* album.

33. The 3.45pm Worksop to Nottingham is hauled by class 4 2-6-4T no. 42185, but the date is unknown. There had been several different signal boxes here. Warsop Junction lost its signal box on 30th January 1983. (R.Humm coll.)

ELMTON & CRESWELL

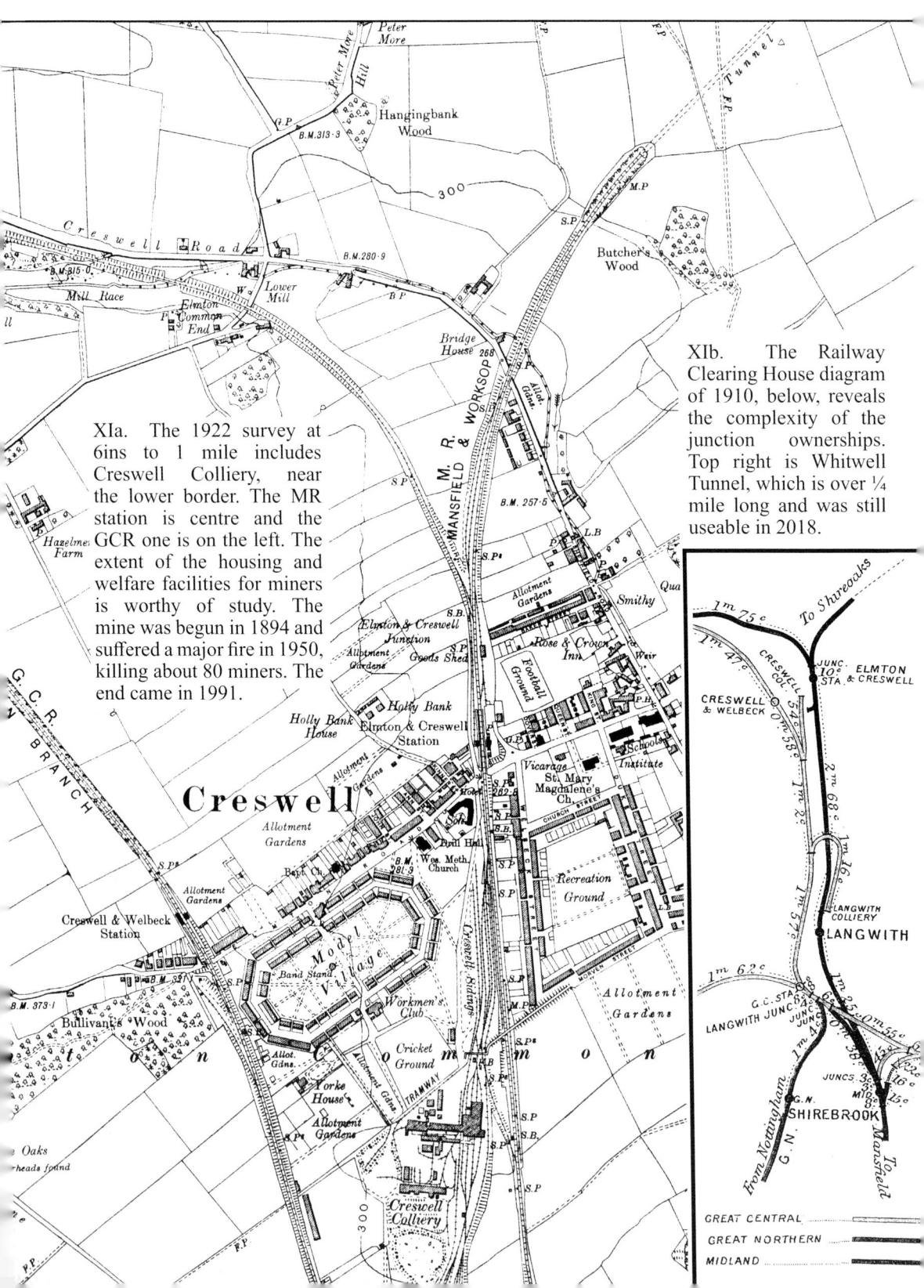

XIa. The 1922 survey at 6ins to 1 mile includes Creswell Colliery, near the lower border. The MR station is centre and the GCR one is on the left. The extent of the housing and welfare facilities for miners is worthy of study. The mine was begun in 1894 and suffered a major fire in 1950, killing about 80 miners. The end came in 1991.

XIb. The Railway Clearing House diagram of 1910, below, reveals the complexity of the junction ownerships. Top right is Whitwell Tunnel, which is over ¼ mile long and was still useable in 2018.

34. The station was named CRESSWELL from its opening with the line until 10th April 1886, when it also received the prefix ELMTON. This postcard carried the original name and so is very early. The view is northwards and includes the goods yard, which closed on 6th January 1964. (P.Laming coll.)

35. A sharp record from 10th May 1952 includes the water tank and two young observers. The 4-4-2T is no. 41961, which was built for the London Tilbury & Southend Railway. It is pulling the 3.40pm Worksop to Nottingham service. (Milepost 92½)

36. The 3.11pm Nottingham to Worksop on 17th March 1962 was headed by class 4 2-6-4T no. 42222. Passenger traffic ceased from 12th October 1964 until 25th May 1998, when two new platforms on the Robin Hood Line came into use. They reopened under the name Creswell (Derbys). (R.Humm coll.)

Elmton & Creswell Junction

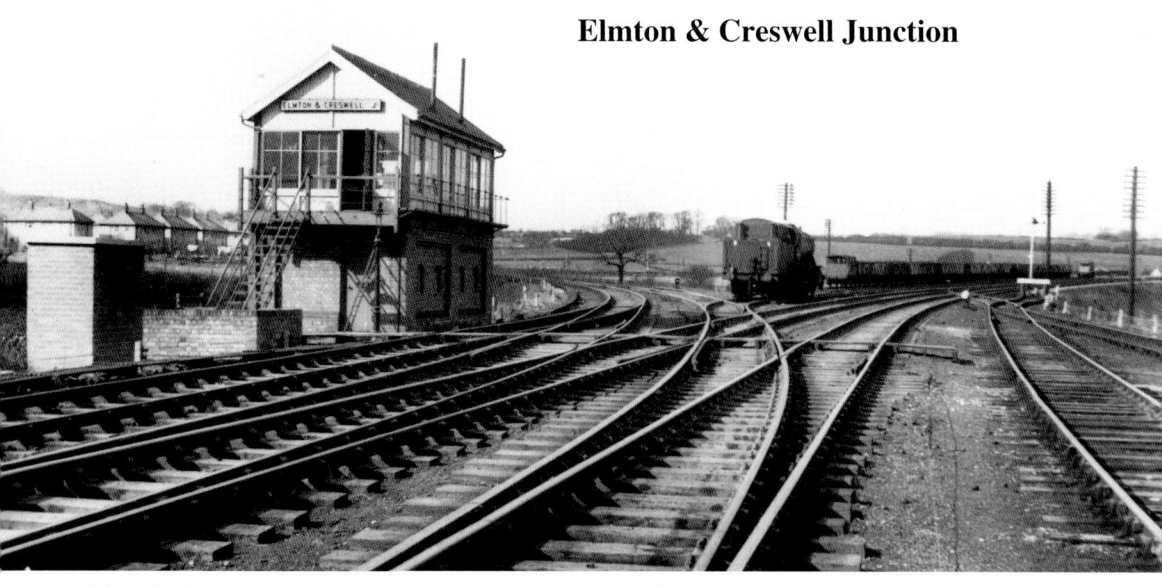

37. The location is clear on the previous two maps. This northward panorama is from 23rd June 1964 and features ex-WD 2-8-0 no. 90290 shunting. On the left is the route to Staveley and Barrow Hill, while our line to Shireoaks is on the right. (Milepost 92½)

38. The driver of no. 58039 receives the single line Tyer's tablet for the Clowne Branch on 27th October 1987. The LMS had provided the signal box in 1946, to replace two MR boxes. The box had a 48-lever frame and it was still standing in 2017, although out of use, as was the single line to Seymour Junction. The box was switched out on 24th April 2010. (R.J.Stewart-Smith)

SOUTH OF WHITWELL

Whitwell Quarry

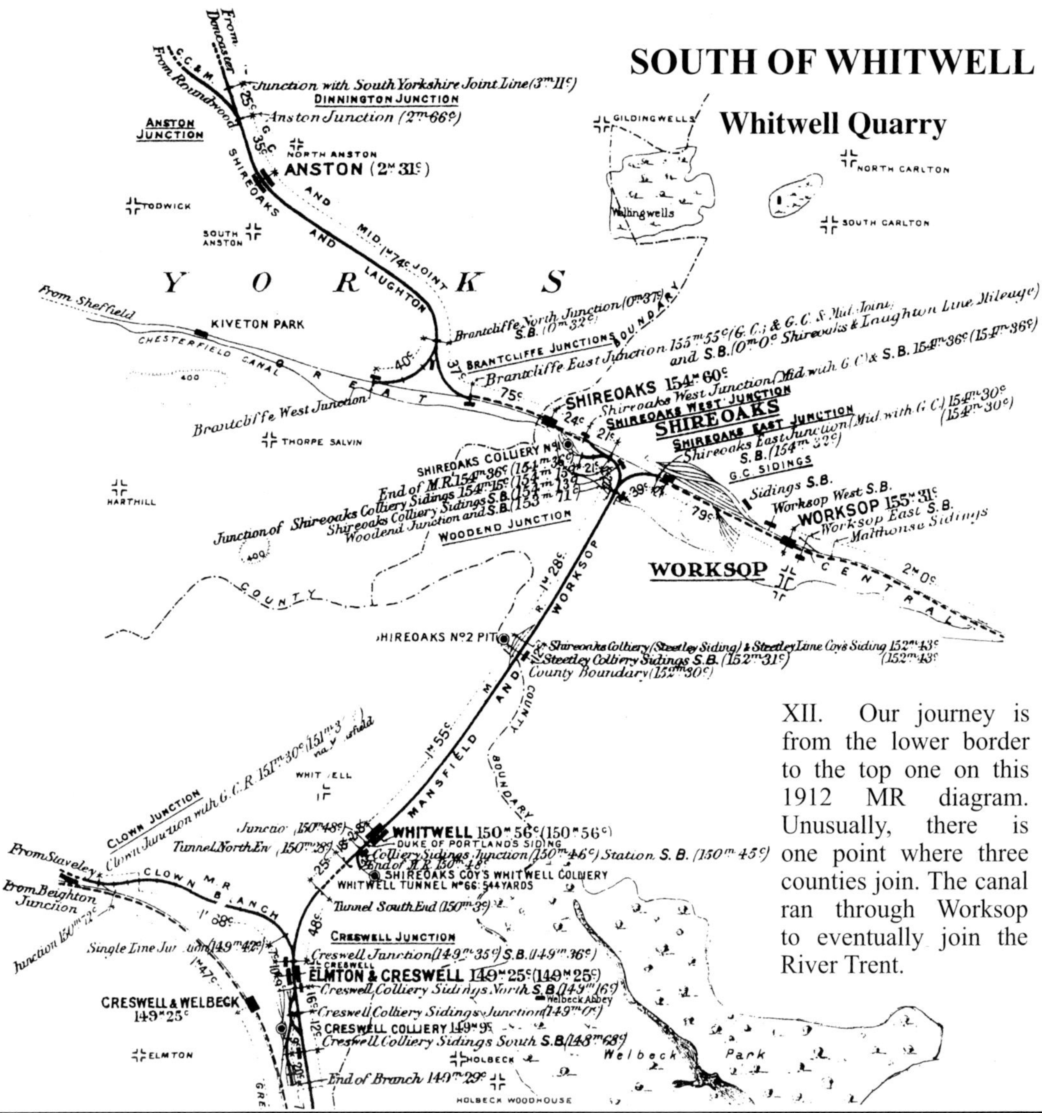

XII. Our journey is from the lower border to the top one on this 1912 MR diagram. Unusually, there is one point where three counties join. The canal ran through Worksop to eventually join the River Trent.

39. Loading is about to start at Whitwell Quarry on 17th August 1990, after the arrival of no. 56058 and its empty wagons from Toton. This was a then recently acquired flow of limestone to Witton, near Birmingham, which ran three times weekly from the Summer of 1990. The siding is shown in the diagram above. (P.D.Shannon)

Whitwell Tunnel

40. Carrying Trainload Construction livery, no. 56058 sets back into the quarry sidings at Whitwell with POA box wagons for loading with limestone on 17th August 1990. The wagons were on hire from Tiger Rail. Visible on the right is the north portal of the 544yd long Whitwell Tunnel. (P.D.Shannon)

41. No. 60015 is seen leaving Whitwell Tunnel on a diverted Kingsbury to Humber empty oil service on 9th August 2015. Diverted due to engineering work between Sheffield and Doncaster on this date, it has taken the route via Toton, then Pye Bridge Junction to Kirkby in Ashfield, where it joined the Robin Hood Line. The track on the left once led into Whitwell Quarry, but had been disused for many years. Oil trains were unusual on this line and were only seen on rare occasions when engineering work prevented them using the normal route. (R.Geach)

XIII. The 1922 survey is shown at 6ins to 1 mile. The station approach road is near the top; access to the goods yard is near the gas works. The mine shaft sinking began in May 1890 and the mining was closely associated with Steetley Colliery, shown in picture 50. Its shaft was used for air intake, while the one here was for bad air uptake. Both could be used for raising coal. This was not an unusual practice, but commonly went under one name. The pits were later linked underground to Shireoaks and use of the shafts could then be changed. The small gas works dates from 1914. Coal would have come by cart across the road. By 1931, the amount was about 1200 tons per annum. Most gas nationwide came from under the North Sea by the early 1970s. It was mostly methane and not deadly carbon monoxide.

42. This view south is from the bridge, which is at the top of the map. The line to the colliery can be seen beyond the empty yard on the left. On the right is the fine house for the station master and the goods shed is in the distance. (P.Laming coll.)

↑ 43. It is 16th February 1957 and class 2 2-6-0 no. 46501 is running through to Worksop prior to working the 12.28pm Saturdays only to Nottingham, which called at all stations. (Milepost 92½)

44. This is the second signal box here; it opened on 14th February 1893. It had a new frame in 1953 and closed on 14th June 1965, when the goods traffic ceased. The date is 28th April 1957. Official closure was on 4th May 1997. (J.Suter)

45. The class 4 2-6-4T was recorded, as no. 42618, but the date was not. Closure to passengers was on 2nd October 1964. The station was dismantled brick by brick in 1981 and rebuilt at Butterley, on the MR demonstration line. The end of the headshunt is on the right. (Milepost 92½)

46. Painted in BR large logo livery, no. 56085 heads south through Whitwell with empty HAA Merry-Go-Round wagons from Cottam Power Station on 13th April 1983. On the right, no. 20026 waits to enter the colliery sidings with a brake van; it would later depart with four wagonloads of coal for Grimsby. Part of the colliery waste tip is on the right. Mining ceased here in June 1986 and demolition was completed by April 1987. The Shireoaks Colliery Company once owned six steam engines: *Edith*, *Jessie*, *Alexandria*, *Duddon*, *Winnie* and *Margaret*. These locos were able to move between the company's collieries, but *Winnie* and *Duddon* were used mostly at Whitwell. (P.D.Shannon)

47. No. 150104 was recorded on a press/driver training run on 6th April 1998, just seven weeks before the reopening of the route as the Robin Hood Line. The headboard was in the classical curvature of a smokebox door. The train ran to Pinxton. (R.J.Stewart-Smith)

48. Whitwell station reopened on 25th May 1998 for the Robin Hood Line extension to Worksop. Unit no. 156413 departs on the 13.40 service from Worksop to Nottingham on 23rd July 2005. The derelict land on the right was once occupied by the station goods yard. Passenger usage annually in 2012-17 averaged 19,000. (P.D.Shannon)

49. No. 47812 is seen on 19th July 2009. The Branch Line Society ran a railtour from Crewe over various freight lines, including the South Yorkshire Joint line, of which the highlights were the lines to Welbeck Colliery and Thoresby. Both these lines are now shut with the trackwork removed on the Welbeck branch. No. 47812 stands at Whitwell where a photographic stop was made from 16.15 to 16.28. Out of view on the rear is no. 66090. The green footbridge was built when the Robin Hood Line reopened in 1998. (R.Geach)

SOUTH OF SHIREOAKS

Steetley Colliery

50. Out of view was the signal box of the name above. It was in use from 1896 to 1985. Coal was not raised here after 1983. (R.Humm coll.)

51. Woodend Junction is just above centre on map XII and the other nearby boxes are marked. Passing on 22nd August 1964 is class 4 2-6-4T no. 42221 working the 3.20pm Saturdays Only Nottingham to Worksop. The signals confirm that it is turning east. (R.Humm coll.)

52. This was the second signal box here and it was open from 9th February 1904 until 25th September 1966. The sidings were in use from 8th January 1893. The photograph is from 14th August 1965, after vandalism. (R.Humm)

Shireoaks Colliery

53. The colliery sidings were accessed from the main line east of the triangular junction, which is beyond the bridge, on the left. The pit was worked from 1859 to 1990. By 1913, there were 717 working underground and 216 on the surface, producing around 1m tons of coal, each year. (R.J.Stewart-Smith)

XIV. The 1949 issue at 5 miles to 1ins has West Junction lower right and, on the left, a tunnel under the Chesterfield Canal, built originally for a tramway. South of this is the limestone quarry and north of it the lime works. They were linked by a 2ft 5ins gauge railway. This was rope-worked, but a new Ruston diesel loco came in 1942. It was out of use by 1957. A standard gauge shunter was on their records. The business was under the name of Steetley.

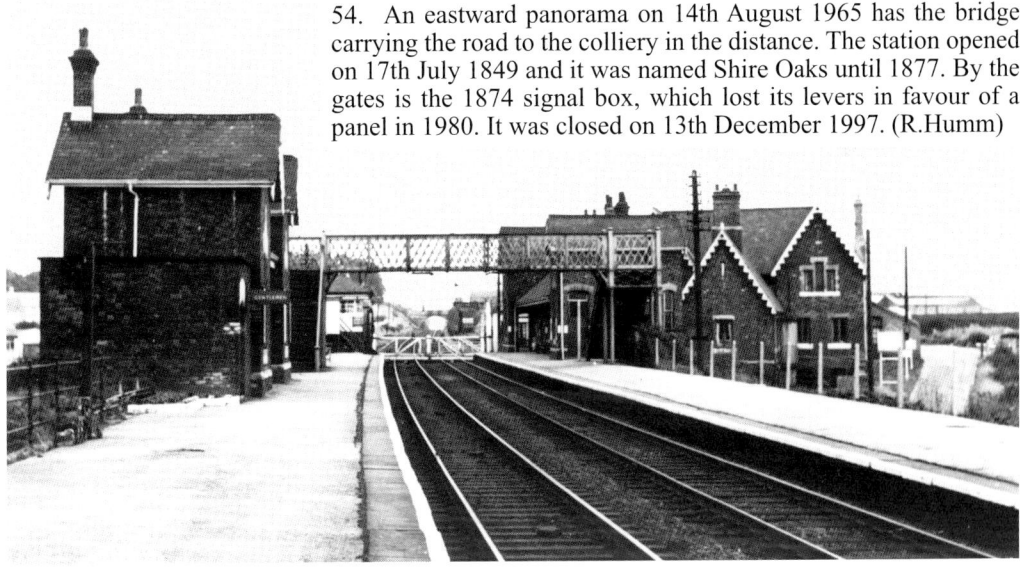

54. An eastward panorama on 14th August 1965 has the bridge carrying the road to the colliery in the distance. The station opened on 17th July 1849 and it was named Shire Oaks until 1877. By the gates is the 1874 signal box, which lost its levers in favour of a panel in 1980. It was closed on 13th December 1997. (R.Humm)

55. Seen on the same day, the fine building ceased to be staffed on 29th June 1969, but trains still called in 2018. The goods yard ceased to be used on 9th December 1963. It had a 5-ton capacity crane for many years. (R.Humm)

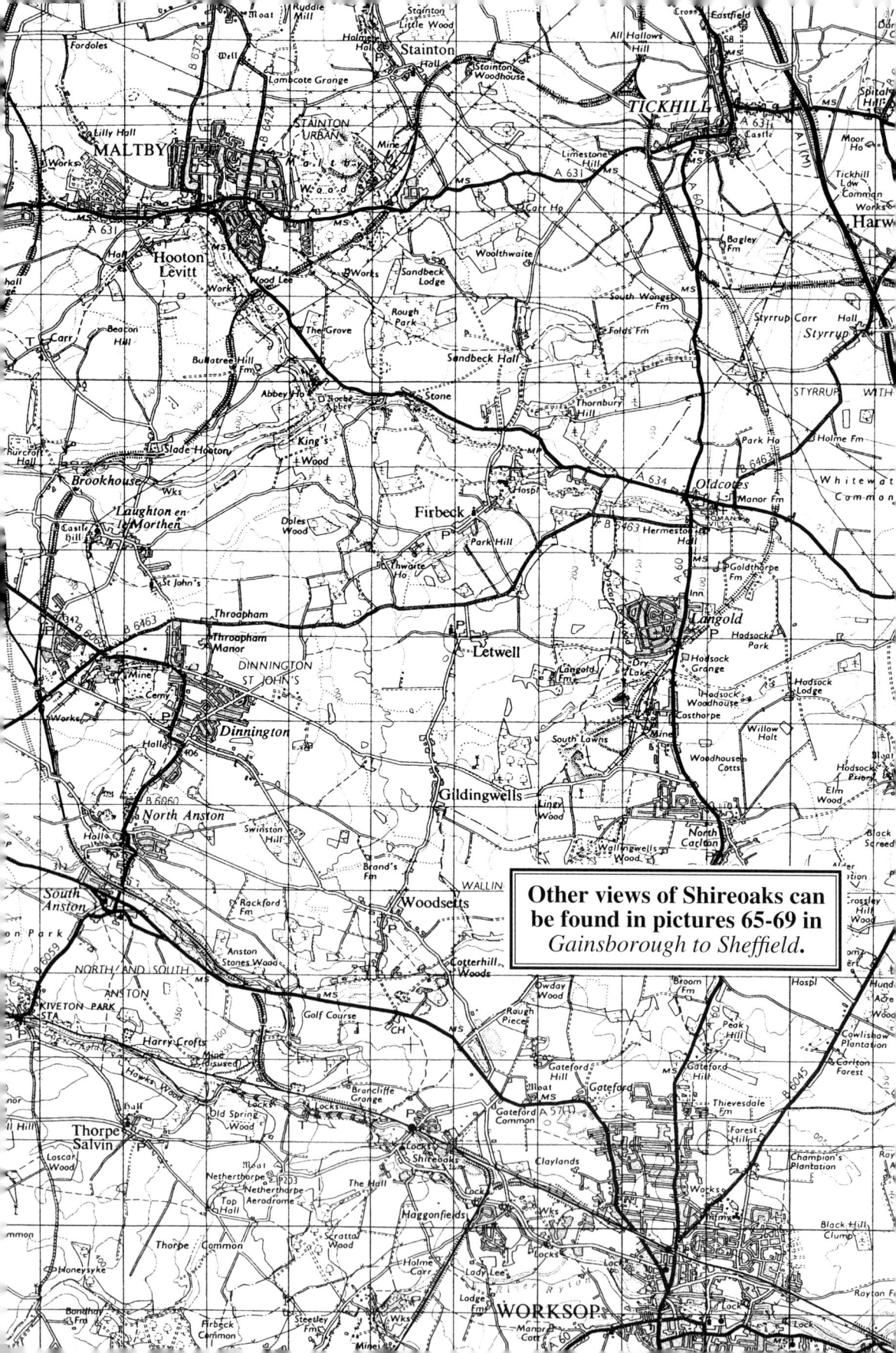

ANSTON

← XV. Our journey continues from the lower border of this 1961 map, scaled at 1ins to 1 mile. We pass the mine near Steetley Farm, turn north near a lock and enter Shireoaks station. Passing more locks, we turn north again aiming for Tickhill, top right. Its station is on the continuation, before picture 61. The line from left to right is the ex-GCR route of 1849, from Woodhouse to Retford. Anston station had been below the word 'Hall'.

56. The station was open from 20th May 1912 to June 1921, October 1921 to April 1926 and July 1927 to December 1929. A few trains called later for works outings. The single siding handled goods traffic until 4th December 1950. (V.Mitchell coll.)

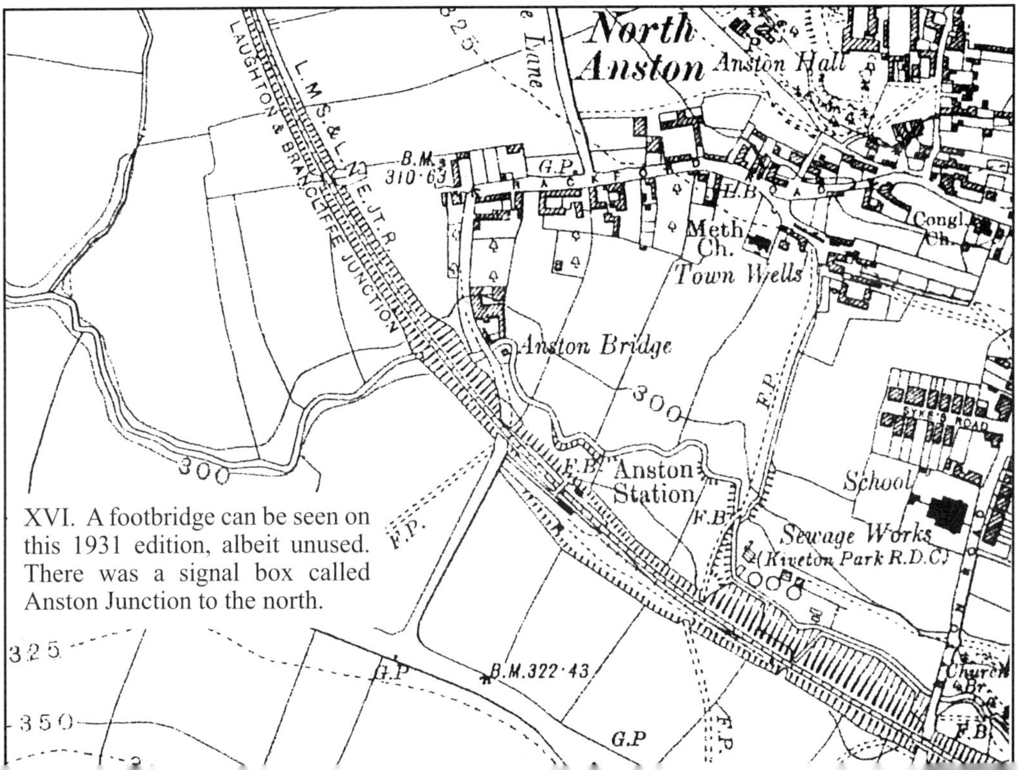

XVI. A footbridge can be seen on this 1931 edition, albeit unused. There was a signal box called Anston Junction to the north.

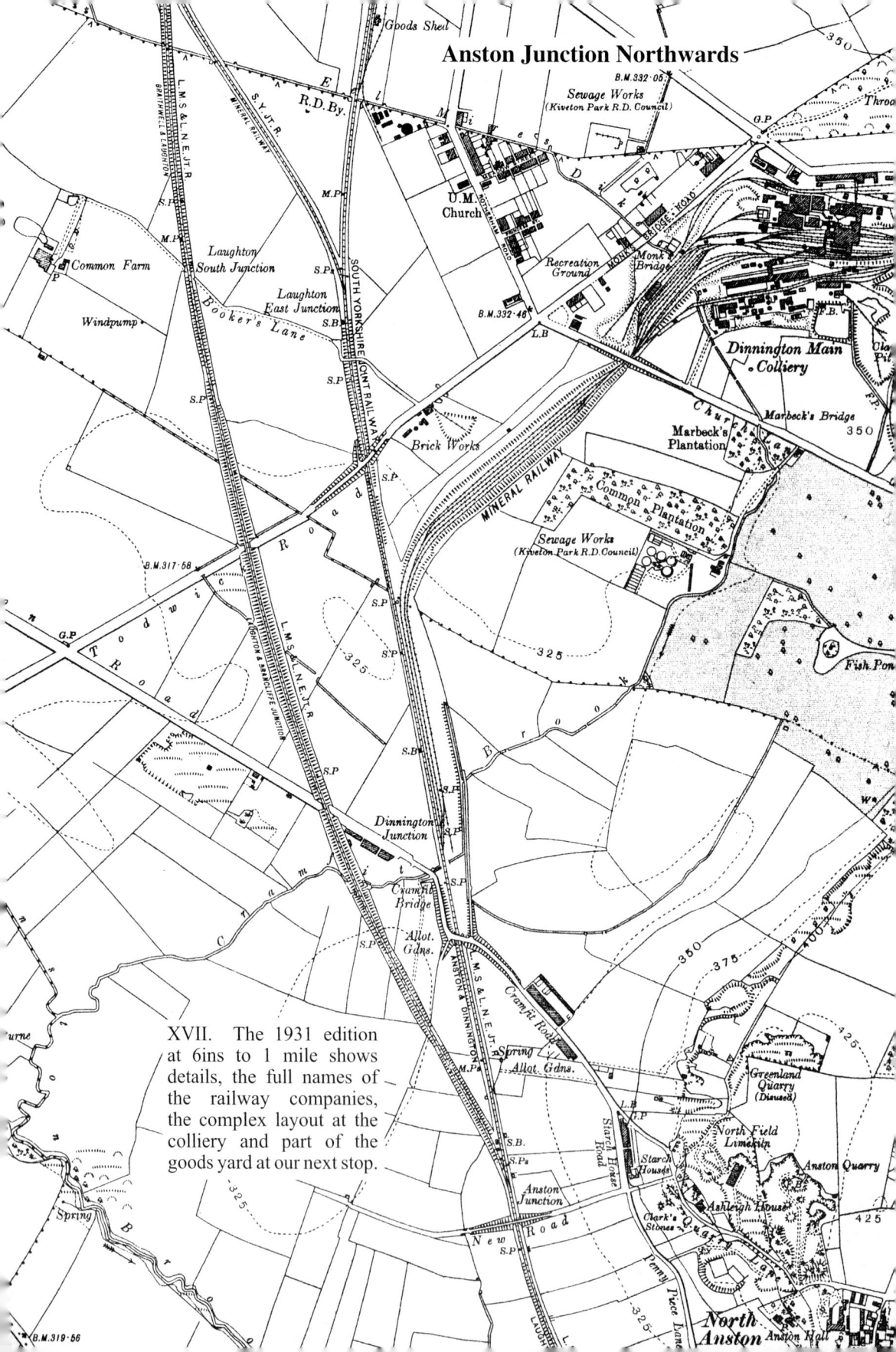

XVII. The 1931 edition at 6ins to 1 mile shows details, the full names of the railway companies, the complex layout at the colliery and part of the goods yard at our next stop.

Dinnington Main Colliery

57. Many of the reception sidings are included in this view north on 20th February 1965. Dinnington Colliery signal box was open from 1907 until 29th November 1997. (R.Humm coll.)

58. Named *Bill*, this 1924 Avonside 0-6-0T was photographed outside its shed at Dinnington Main Colliery on 30th May 1968. Sinking began in 1902 and the two shafts began work in 1904. Production ceased in 1992. (A.J.Booth)

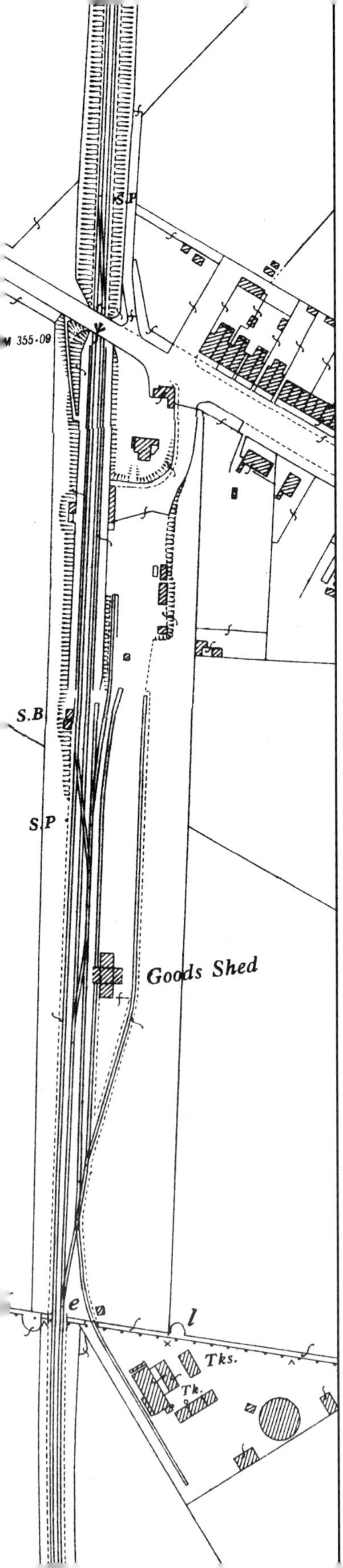

DINNINGTON & LAUGHTON

← XVIII. The 1930 survey includes some recent terraces for use by miners, all with privies in their gardens. A road runs down to the main station building and a path serves the other platform. Lower right is the small local gas works.

59. The station was open from 1st December 1910 to April 1926 and from July 1927 to 2nd December 1929. There were occasional special trains recorded thereafter. There are no nameboards, lights or signals and, thus, we presume that this view north is prior to the opening. (J.Alsop coll.)

60. Another view north, but this is on 20th February 1965. This is Dinnington Station box, which was at the north end of the double track from Brancliffe Junction. It was abolished in 1973, but the other buildings vanished about 10 years earlier. The goods yard was in use until 3rd May 1965. (R.Humm coll.)

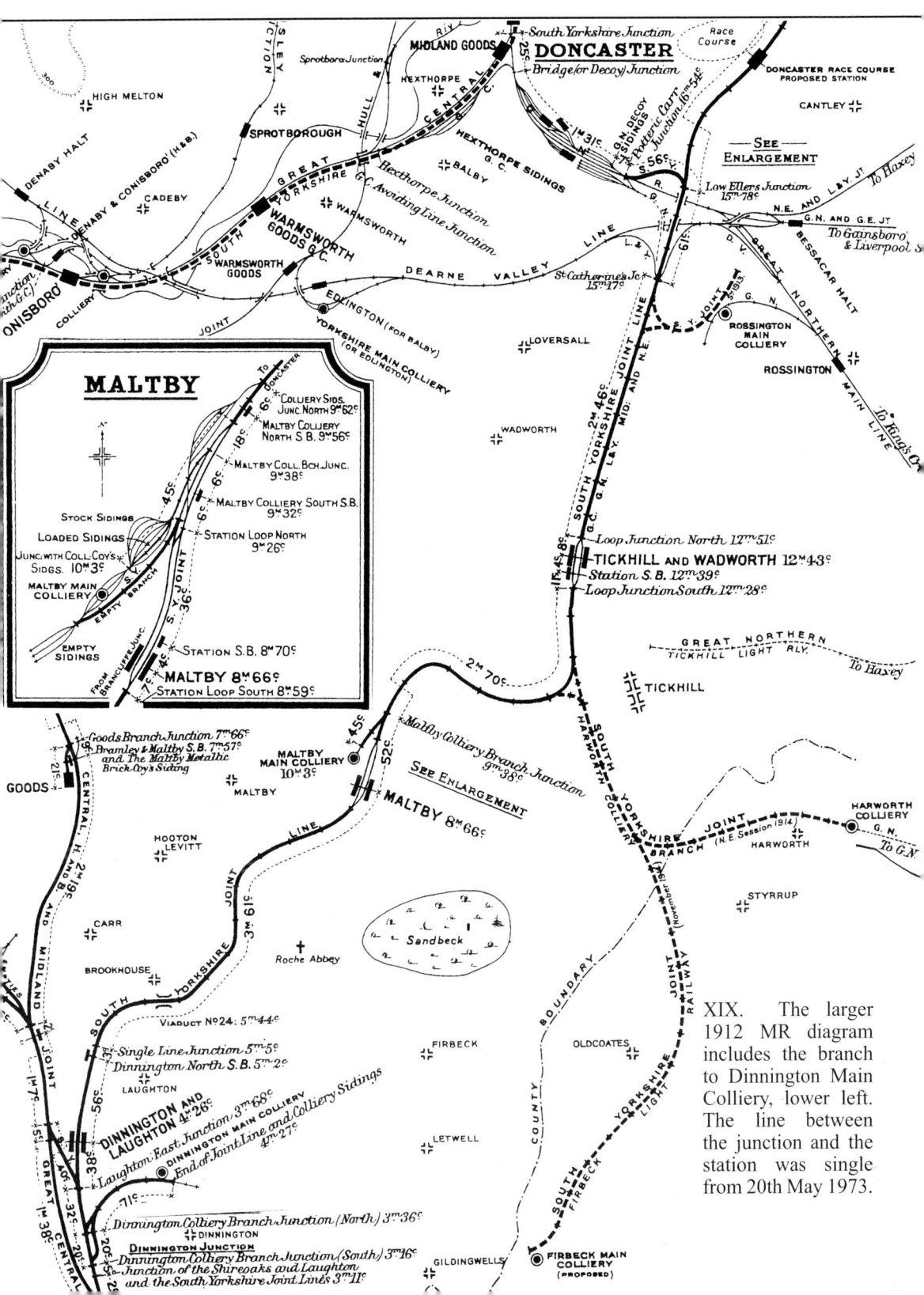

XIX. The larger 1912 MR diagram includes the branch to Dinnington Main Colliery, lower left. The line between the junction and the station was single from 20th May 1973.

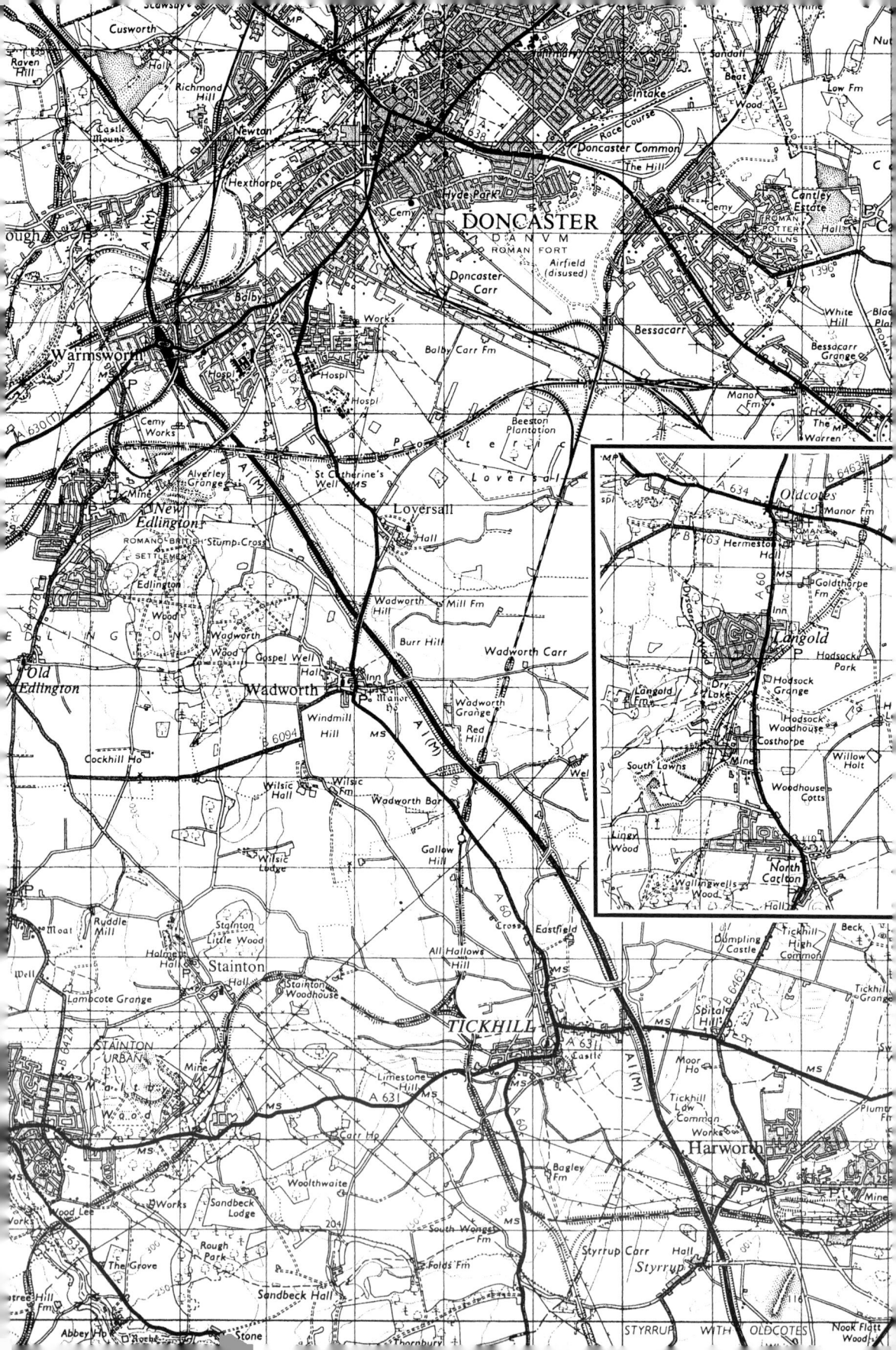

XX. The 1961 edition at 1ins to 1 mile has the station east of the town, lower left. Tickhill station is north of its town. One of the first motorways is shown as A1(M). Inset is the continuation of the line to Firbeck Colliery from the lower border. It was built under a Light Railway Order of 22nd February 1916.

61. This is a northward panorama from the early years. The station opened on 1st December 1910, although the 1901 census had shown only 716 residents. Due to mining, the figures grew greatly, reaching 14,300 by 1961. (P.Laming coll.)

62. Part of the goods yard is evident in this slightly later view. It had a 5-ton crane and remained in use until 14th June 1965. The passenger dates are those shown in caption 59. Maltby Colliery North Box closed on 19th February 1978. (J.Alsop coll.)

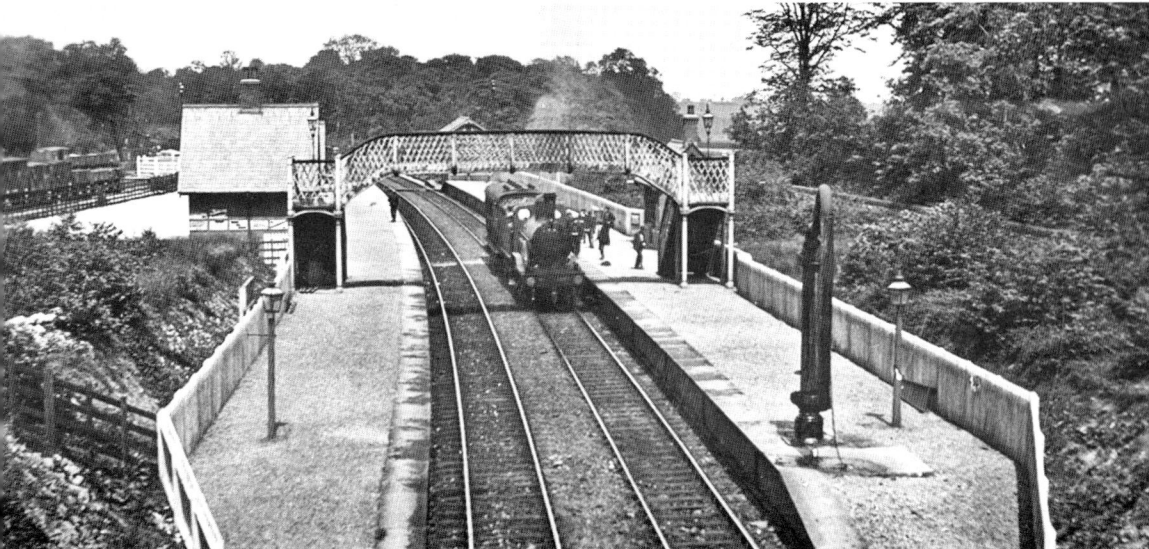

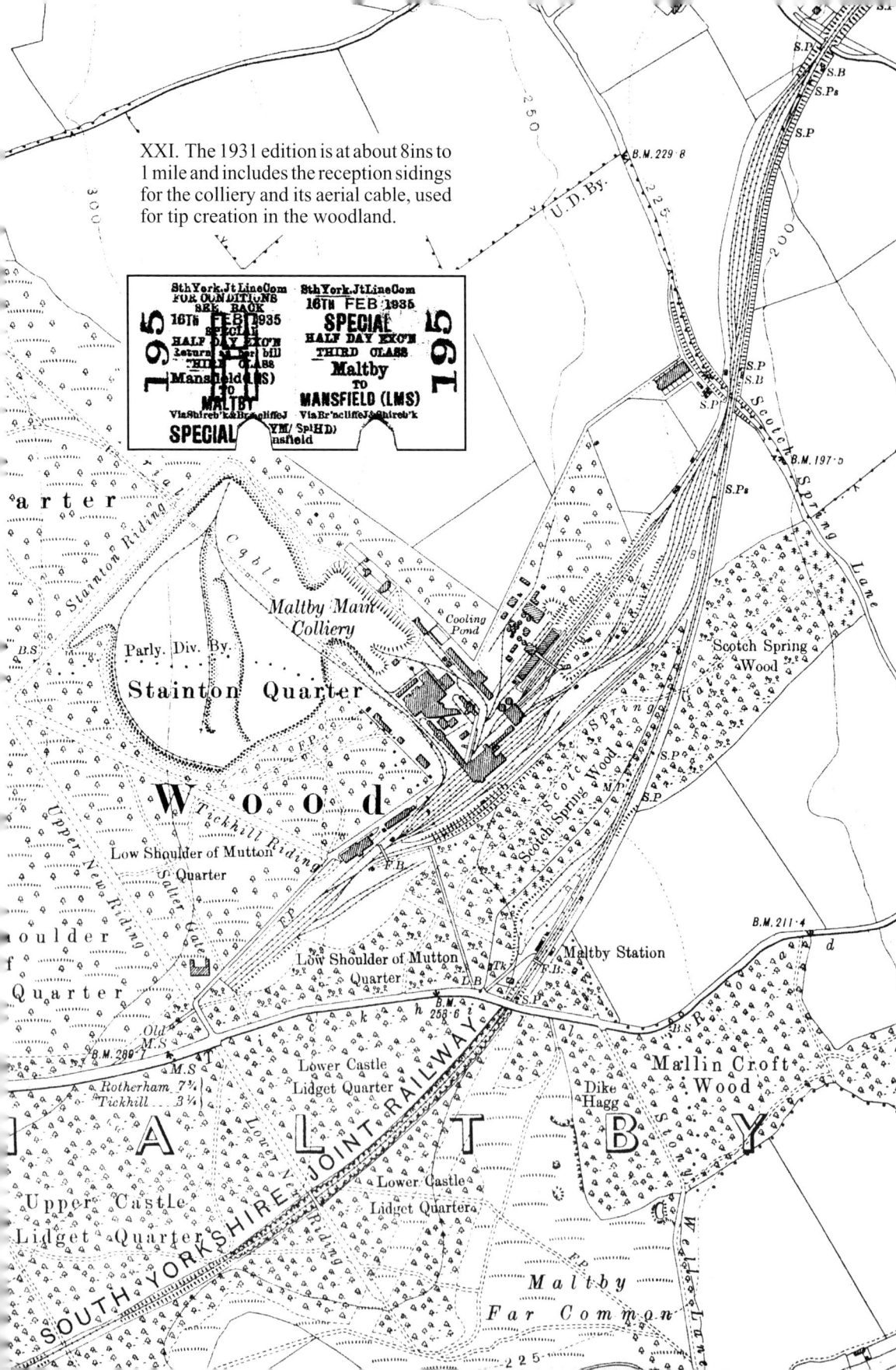

XXI. The 1931 edition is at about 8ins to 1 mile and includes the reception sidings for the colliery and its aerial cable, used for tip creation in the woodland.

63. Another early view, but this gives architectural details, plus the location of the cattle pens. The ballasting and platform surfacing are impeccable. White edging of platforms did not arrive until the black-out of World War II. No. 244 looks like a very elderly MSLR 0-4-4T. On the right is the signal box, which was open until 26th November 1962. (J.Alsop coll.)

64. All was remarkably intact on 12th May 1957 when an RCTS railtour called the 'East Midlander No.3' stopped. It ran from Nottingham to York, via Rotherham, and is seen on the return journey behind no. 62571, a class D16 4-4-0. A few Summer Saturday trains had called here until 1937. (D.K.Jones)

65. The GCR buildings were known as the 'Double Pavilion' style and this example was recorded on 26th May 1975. It was used by a firm of builders for many years. The goods yard had closed on 14th June 1965. (N.D.Mundy)

NORTH OF MALTBY

Maltby Main Colliery

66. The location of the colliery and its extent are shown on the previous two maps. This and the next view are from February 1989. Over 500 were still employed here in 2007 on mine-related matters. This is Maltby Colliery South box, which opened on 12th June 1911. It still controlled the passing loop in 2018, but was devoid of 'South' in its name. (R.J.Stewart-Smith)

67. Sinking of shafts began in 1910 and over 400 houses were built for the workers. All faces were being worked by 1914, but an explosion in 1923 killed 27 men. Closure came in 2013 and demolition took place in the following year. (R.J.Stewart-Smith)

← 68. Moving on, we reach North Box, which still retained its foot boards and hand rails for the benefit of those cleaning its windows. It is 26th May 1975 and the standard water butt has gone, but its supply pipe remains. (N.D.Mundy)

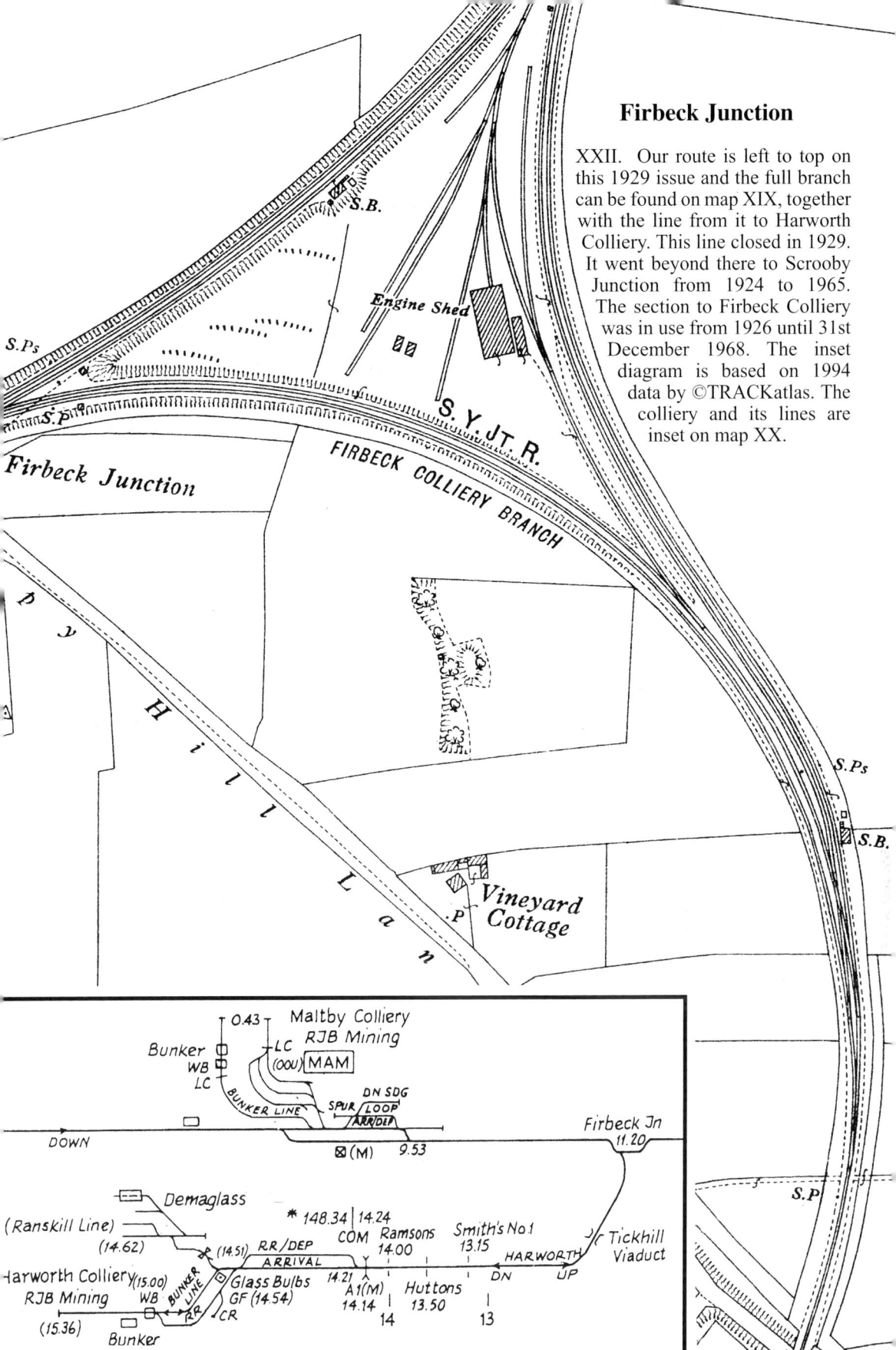

69. Box A is top left on the map and has modern flat bottom rails nearby. It was in use from 1st October 1926 until 7th October 1984 and is seen on 26th May 1975. (N.D.Mundy)

70. Box B is on the right of the map, but the photo date is unknown. The other junctions were termed East and West, but this one was always just 'B'. It closed on 8th August 1983. (R.Humm coll.)

Harworth Colliery

71. The extent of the sidings is shown lower right on map XX. Shaft sinking began in 1913, but production was delayed until 1924. Requisitioned from the German owners of Harworth Colliery at the outbreak of war in August 1914, this Hohenzollern 0-6-0WT is seen shunting there on 30th April 1955. (B.Mettam/IRS coll.)

72. From about 1932 to 1958 the coking plant at Harworth, adjacent to the colliery, was shunted by a variety of locomotives on short-term hire. On 30th April 1955, the duty locomotive was this 1921 Manning Wardle 0-6-0ST, which had begun life helping build a harbour at Bombay. (B.Mettam/IRS coll.)

73. The last two locomotives to shunt Harworth Colliery were this pair of Thomas Hill diesel hydraulic ones, photographed there on 6th August 1977. The old headgears were replaced in 1989 and 1994. In 1993, the mine had just exceeded 1m tons of coal raised in one year. (A.J.Booth)

74. Nos 20208 and 20133 depart with a local trip freight to Worksop on 13th April 1983. The train is carrying domestic coal in vacuum-braked MCV wagons, which would soon be taken out of service, as BR switched to air-braked stock. The sidings also hold two rakes of air-braked HBA manual-discharge hoppers and two rakes of air-braked HAA MGR hoppers. The single track on the right gave access to Harworth Glass Bulbs factory; it had once formed part of a through route to the East Coast main line. Mining ended here in 2006. (P.D.Shannon)

75. The vast extent of the site can be appreciated in this panorama from 31st July 1984. The new loading gear is horizontal in the background. Much of the coal went to Drax and Cottam for power production. Demolition took place in 2016 and housing followed. (R.J.Stewart-Smith)

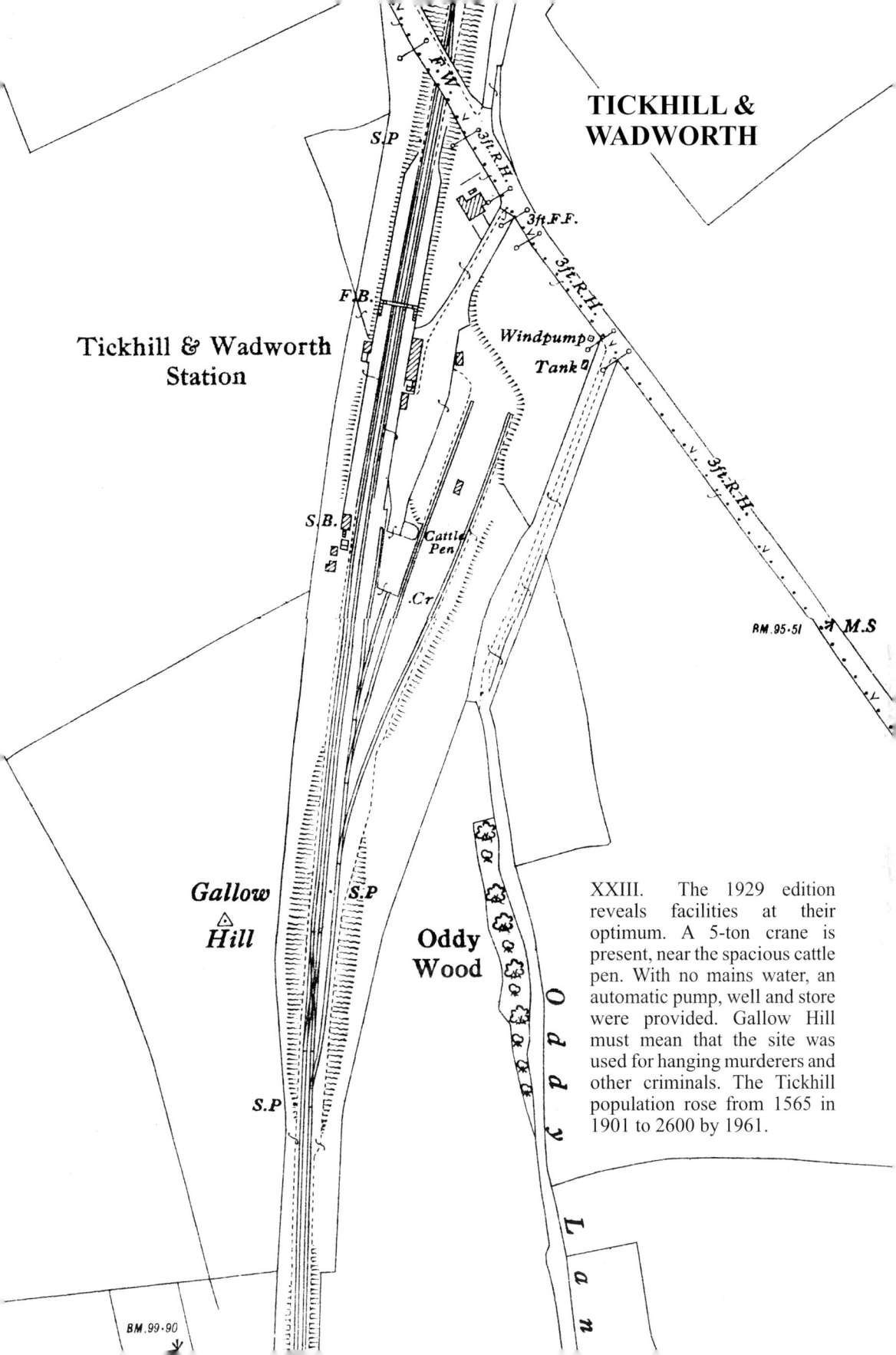

XXIII. The 1929 edition reveals facilities at their optimum. A 5-ton crane is present, near the spacious cattle pen. With no mains water, an automatic pump, well and store were provided. Gallow Hill must mean that the site was used for hanging murderers and other criminals. The Tickhill population rose from 1565 in 1901 to 2600 by 1961.

76. This is the unopened station in 1908, devoid of lights and pen fencing in the foreground. On the right appears to be a standard weighbridge office, but no W.M. appears on the map. However, there is one on the 1962 edition. (J.Alsop coll.)

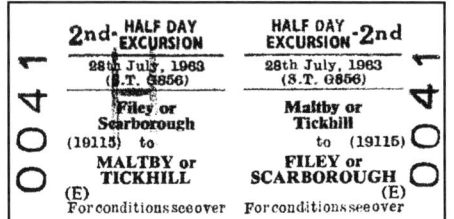 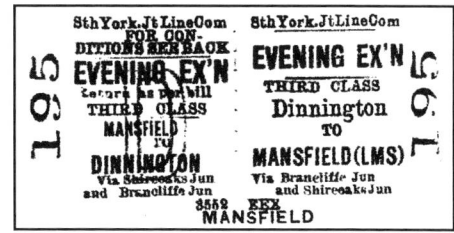

77. This and the next three pictures tell the story. Many company disputes arose and the regular service did not start until 1st December 1910. Bowler hats suggest that important officials were present. The data was scratched into the chemicals on the glass plate negatives. (J.Suter coll.)

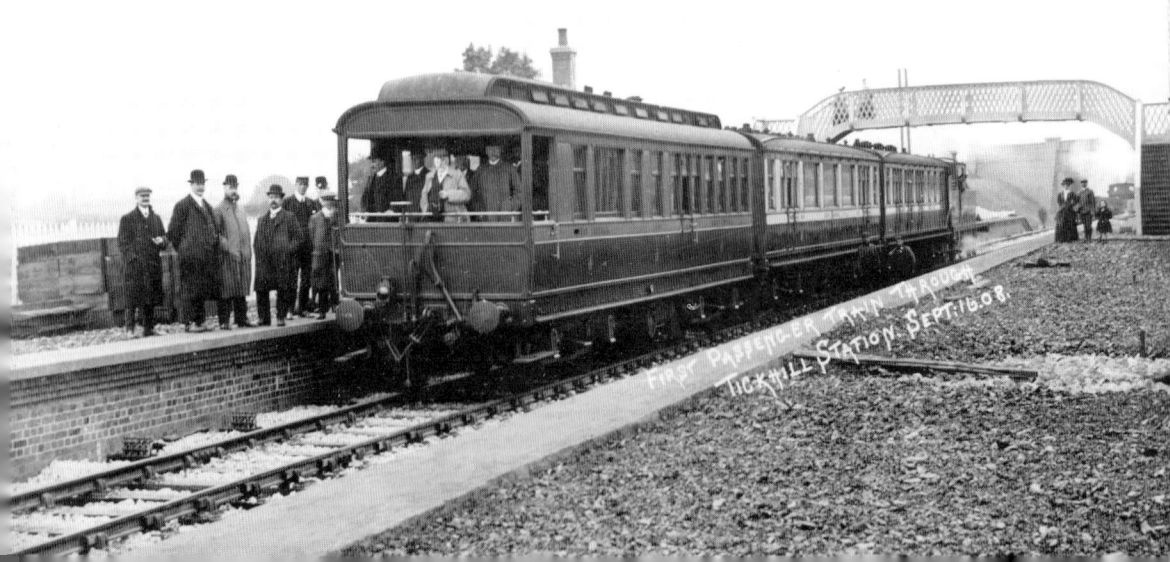

78. This appears to be the same train again, with GCR 4-4-2T no. 1062 leading. The foreground undergrowth seems well-established. There is record of a Sunday School outing train to Cleethorpes on 6th July 1910; a rare treat. (P.Laming coll.)

79. Eleven six-wheeled coaches with GCR by the guard's left elbow form a rare picture of the official regular train on 1st December 1910. For the first 12 months the service was a joint operation with the GNR, but they then resigned after the disputes. (J.Suter coll.)

80. Minutes later, the cameraman had moved his tripod to the other end of the train to dwell on GCR 4-4-0 no. 688. The consortium of five companies was known as the South Yorkshire Joint Railway; GNR, GCR, LYR, MR and NER. (J.Alsop coll.)

81. The cattle wagons appear to be carrying horses and are being unloaded in sequences. The name *Wadworth* had been added on 1st July 1911 and it was retained to the end. The station was closed temporarily between April 1926 and April 1927 after a bacterial infection outbreak, due to horse faeces, locally. Maybe ticks were still sucking blood nearby. (J.Suter coll.)

← 82. The signal box was in use until 3rd May 1970. It is seen opposite on 13th June 1959. Regular passenger trains had ceased on 8th July 1929, but the goods yard was in use until 2nd November 1964. Only the station house and one track remained in 2018. Both were still usable. (Milepost 92½)

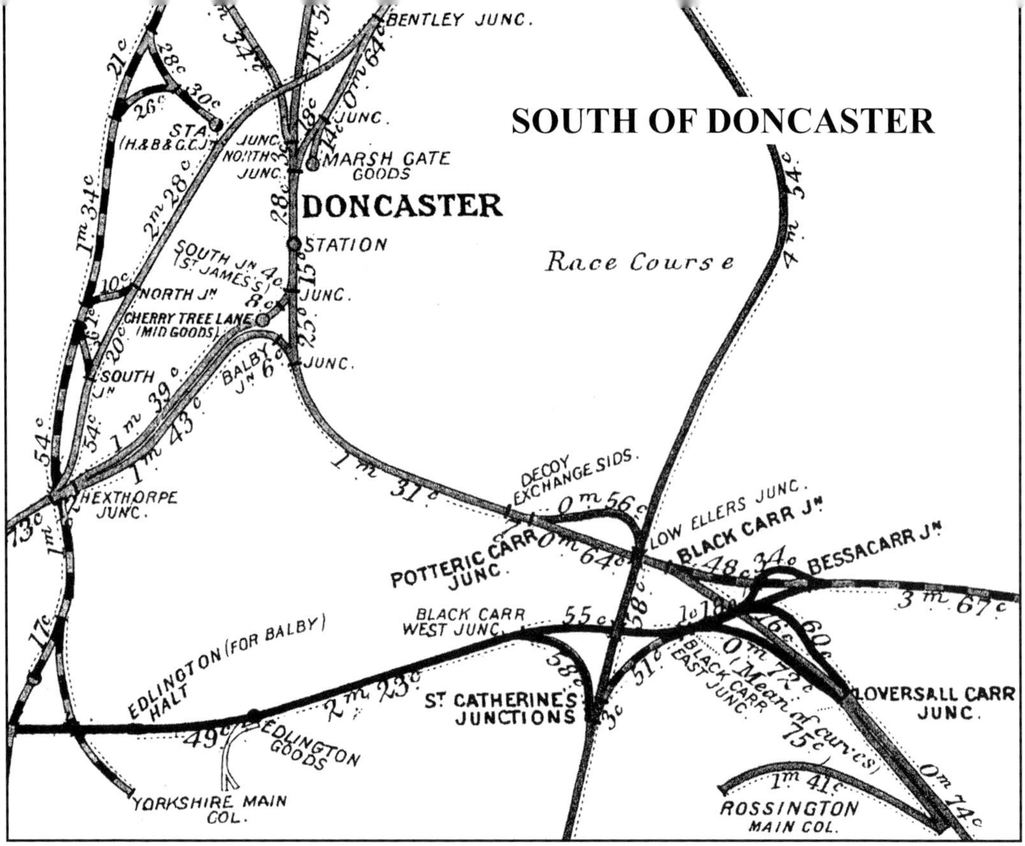

XXIV. The 1920 Railway Clearing House diagram has the route from Tickhill lower centre. Most freight trains from it for the north would pass the Race Course. Not all the junctions are named.

St. Catherine's Junction

83. This is the first junction in the complex and is at the bottom of the map. The signal box was taken out of use on 2nd May 1977. (N.D.Mundy)

Low Ellers Junction

84. This is the next junction north, where passenger trains using our route would turn left. The curve between here and Potteric Carr Junction came into use in 1909, ready for SYJR trains. (N.D.Mundy)

Potteric Carr Junction

85. The figure 5 refers to the speed limit. The 1909 signal box had 36 levers and was photographed on 7th March 1979; it was closed on 21st May of that year. (N.D.Mundy)

Decoy Signal Boxes

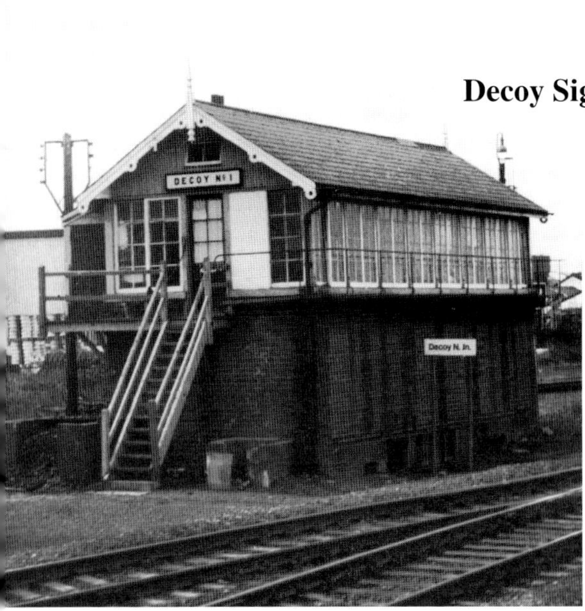

Bridge Junction

←*(far left)*   86. Decoy No. 1 box had 95 levers and remained operational from 1895 until 1979. Decoy Bank can be found on the next map. (N.D.Mundy)

←   87. The two yards of Decoy Sidings are on the right of the next map, near Decoygates. The main lines separate them. No. 2 had 100 levers and functioned between 1895 and 1979 also. (N.D.Mundy)

88. This northward panorama is from Balby Road Bridge, which is annotated on the left of the next map. It also marks the position of the church. The four main running lines are in front of Bridge Junction signal box. It had 30 levers and was in use from 1st May 1878 to 7th July 1979. No. 47462 is working the 12.55 Bradford to Kings Cross on 27th May 1978. (T.Heavyside)

DONCASTER

XXV. The station and Plant Locomotive Works are top left on this 1904 edition at 4ins to 1 mile. The last steam loco was produced there in 1957 and the last such overhaul was in 1967. An electrification fixed equipment depot was created nearby in 1986. It supplied materials for the main line.

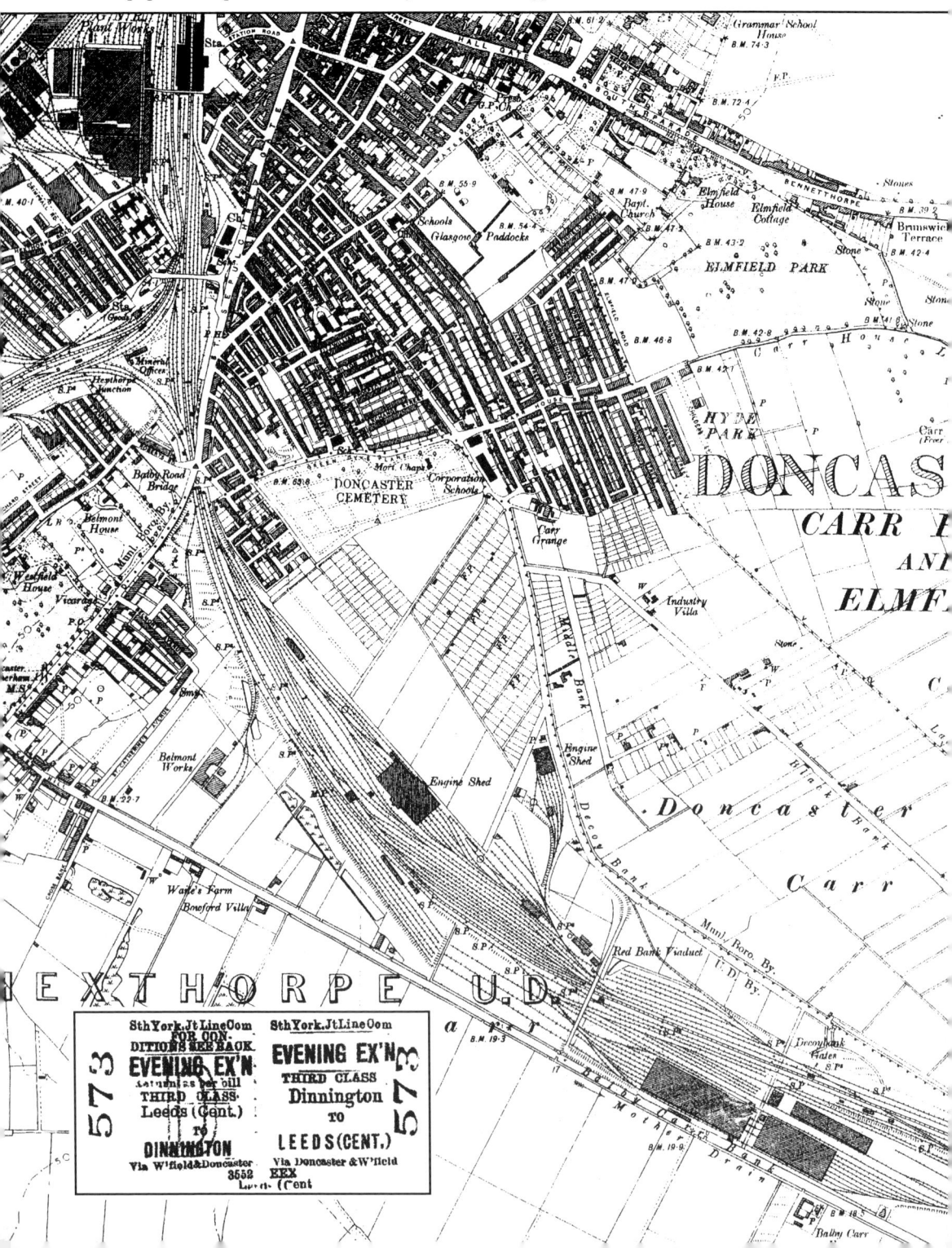

89. Opening in September 1848, the first station was about ½ mile to the north of the lasting site, which was used from September 1850. The eastern facade is seen in the late 19th Century. The signage of the entrance was dominated by its owner, the GNR. The GCR receives a small board, at the left end of the canopy. However, horse droppings clearance would be responsibility of the former. (W.Jenner coll.)

90. Two new through lines were created in 1936 and a one mile extension of the sidings serving the Wheatley Industrial Estate followed in 1938. This 1930s view features LNER no. 6059, a class C13 4-4-2T type, built in 1903-05. (R.Humm coll.)

91. The Plant is top left in this panorama from 27th May 1978 and the staff footbridge to it is passing over all the tracks. The bridge was roofed for many years and its centre was later rebuilt as a raised lattice structure, as seen opposite. No. E51281 is leading the 08.35 Hull to Manchester Piccadilly. (T.Heavyside)

DONCASTER.—**The Albany Temperance Commercial** Hotel. Very Central. Three minutes' walk from the Station Moderate charges. Market Place corner of Baxter Gate.
GEORGE RAITHBY, Proprietor

DONCASTER.—**Fallas** Commercial Temperance Hotel, 20, Hall Gate. Central. Cars pass the door. Moderate Tariff. E. LANSDOWN, Proprietress.

DONCASTER.—
"**WEBB'S HOTEL,**" 19, Hall Gate.

From *Good Lines*, monthly journal of the Temperance Society, dated 1911.

92. On the crossover on 11th May 1999 is no. 60053 with a southbound MGR service, while the 14.30 Edinburgh to Kings Cross waits to depart. The roof line above it is that of the new entrance building, which was started in 1938. Major changes were underway in 2015: platform 0 was added, nos 1, 3, 4 and 8 were for through stopping trains, nos 2 and 5 were south bays and 0, 6 and 7 served as north bays. (P.Barnes)

Other views are in our *Newark to Doncaster* and *Lincoln to Doncaster* albums. These include the locomotive works and engine sheds. *Doncaster Trolleybuses* contains many local images of interest.

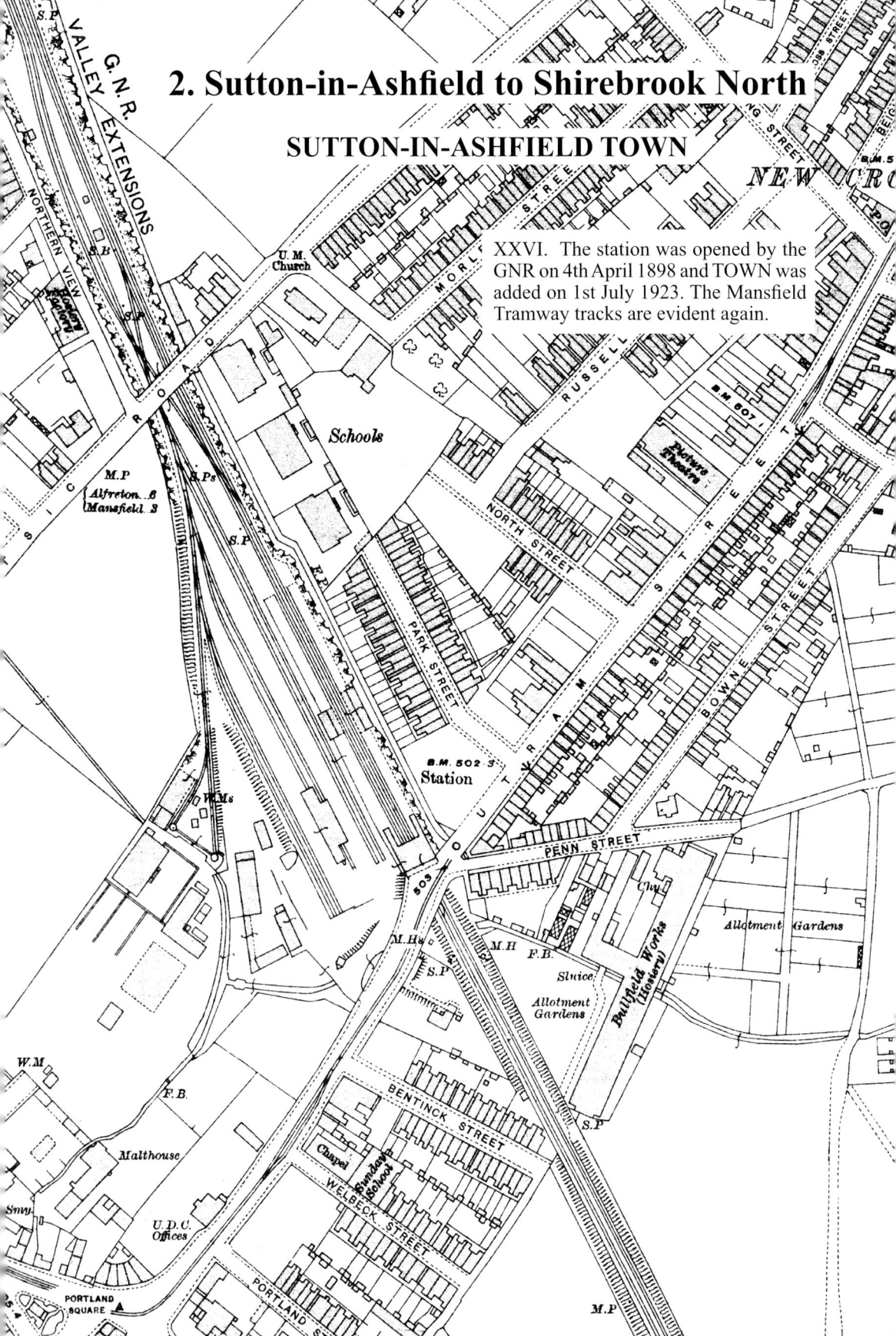

2. Sutton-in-Ashfield to Shirebrook North

SUTTON-IN-ASHFIELD TOWN

XXVI. The station was opened by the GNR on 4th April 1898 and TOWN was added on 1st July 1923. The Mansfield Tramway tracks are evident again.

93. A fine southward presentation is seen soon after the second board carrying FOR HUTHWAITE, which was used in 1907-23. It is behind the seated folk. The station is reported to have had nearly 30 gas lamps. Regular trains ceased to call in 1931, for 25 years. (R.Humm coll.)

94. Running to Nottingham Victoria is no. 67760 a class L1 2-6-4T, a type introduced in 1945. The signal box in the distance had 16 levers. The station reopened on 20th February 1956, but closed to passengers on 17th September 1956 officially. No trains appeared in *Bradshaw* that year. (SLS coll.)

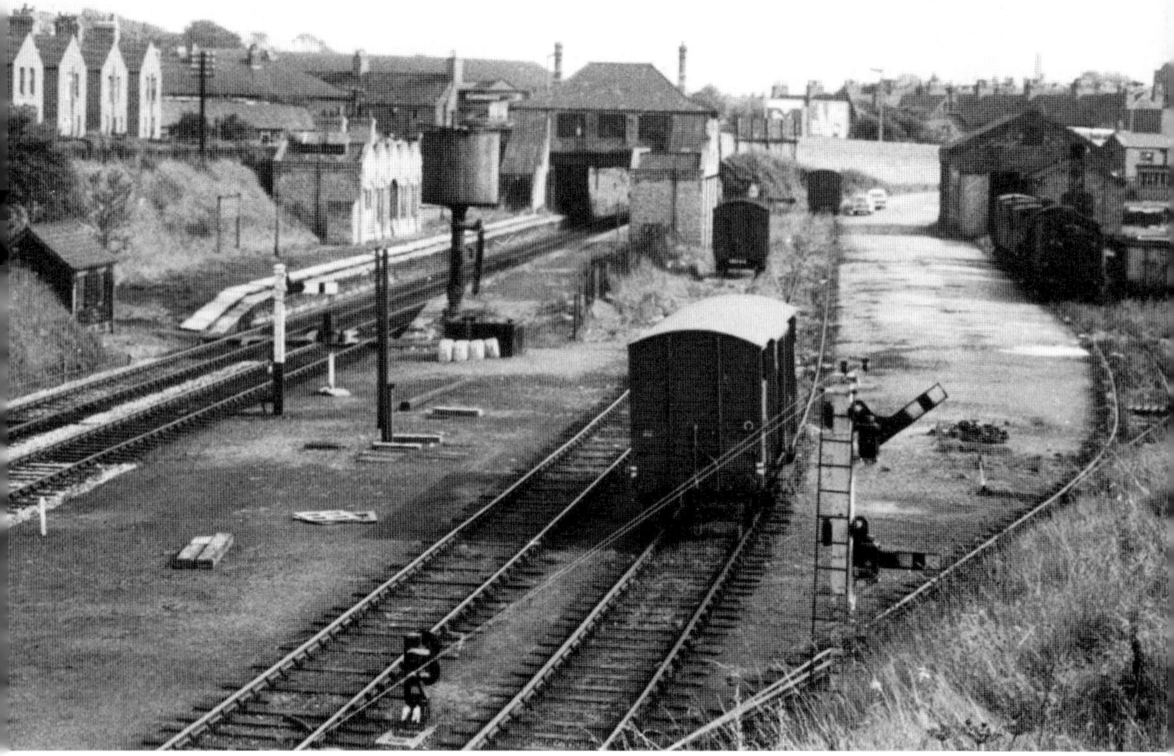

95. This panorama is from 13th August 1965. The goods yard closure came on 1st February 1965. The population had grown from 14,862 in 1901 to 40,680 in 1961. The route closed in 1968. (R.Humm coll.)

MIDLAND RAILWAY. This Ticket is issued subject to the Regulations & Conditions stated in the Company's Time Tables & Bills.
THIRD CLASS. THIRD CLASS.
AVAILABLE ON DAY OF ISSUE ONLY.
Sutton-in-Ashfield to
KIRKBY-IN-ASHFIELD
FARE 2d. FARE 2d.
Sutton-in-A-Kirkby-in-A Sutton-in-A-Kirkby-in-A
2070 3070

MIDLAND RAILWAY. This Ticket is issued subject to the Regulations & Conditions stated in the Company's Time Tables & Bills.
THIRD CLASS. THIRD CLASS.
AVAILABLE ON DAY OF ISSUE ONLY.
Sutton-in-Ashfield to
SUTTON JUNCTION
FARE 1d. FARE 1d.
Sutton in A SuttonJ Sutton-in-A-SuttonJ
3934 3934

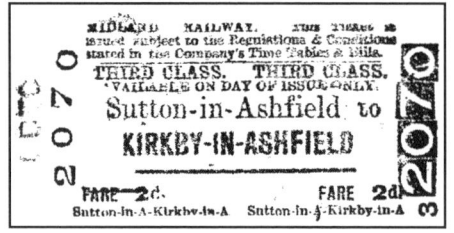

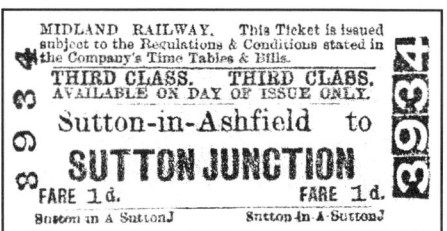

NORTH OF SUTTON-IN-ASHFIELD

Sutton Colliery

96. The branch turns west off our route about one mile north of the station. It was in use from 1897 to about 1914 and thus does not appear on map II. The branch from the 'City of Whiteborough', shown near the left border, served the colliery from 1866 to 1991. It was an MR line until 1923. This shows the pit on its last productive day: 25th August 1989. (R.J.Stewart-Smith)

XXVII. The 6ins to 1 mile issue of 1921 includes a clay pit. Many collieries produced bricks from such surface deposits nearby. Shaft sinking began in 1874 and both were brick lined. An explosion on 21st February 1957 resulted in five fatalities.

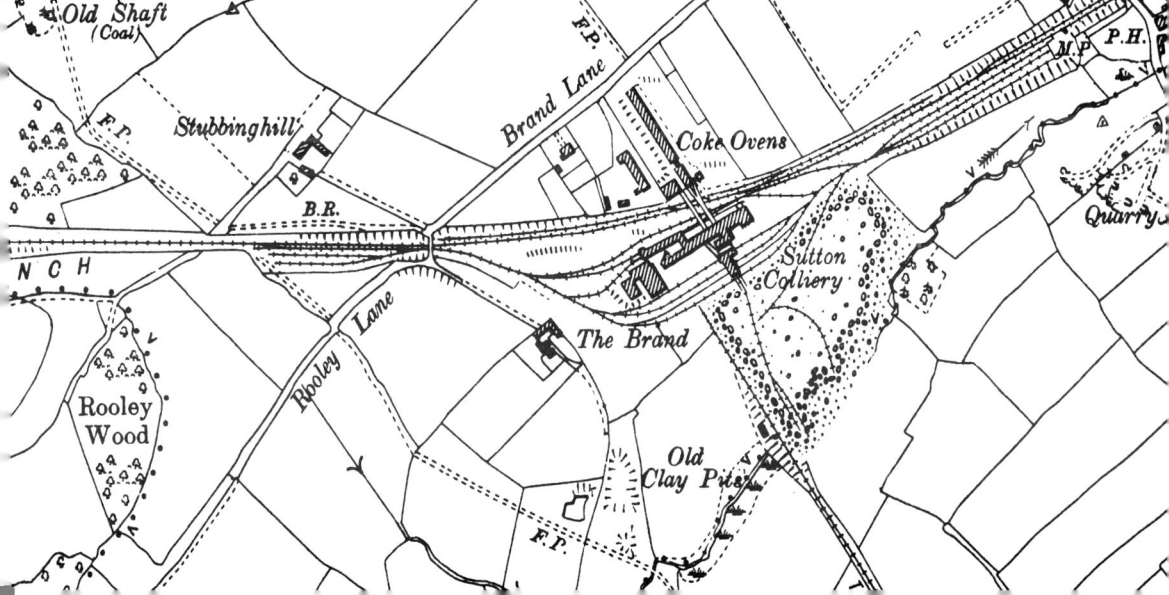

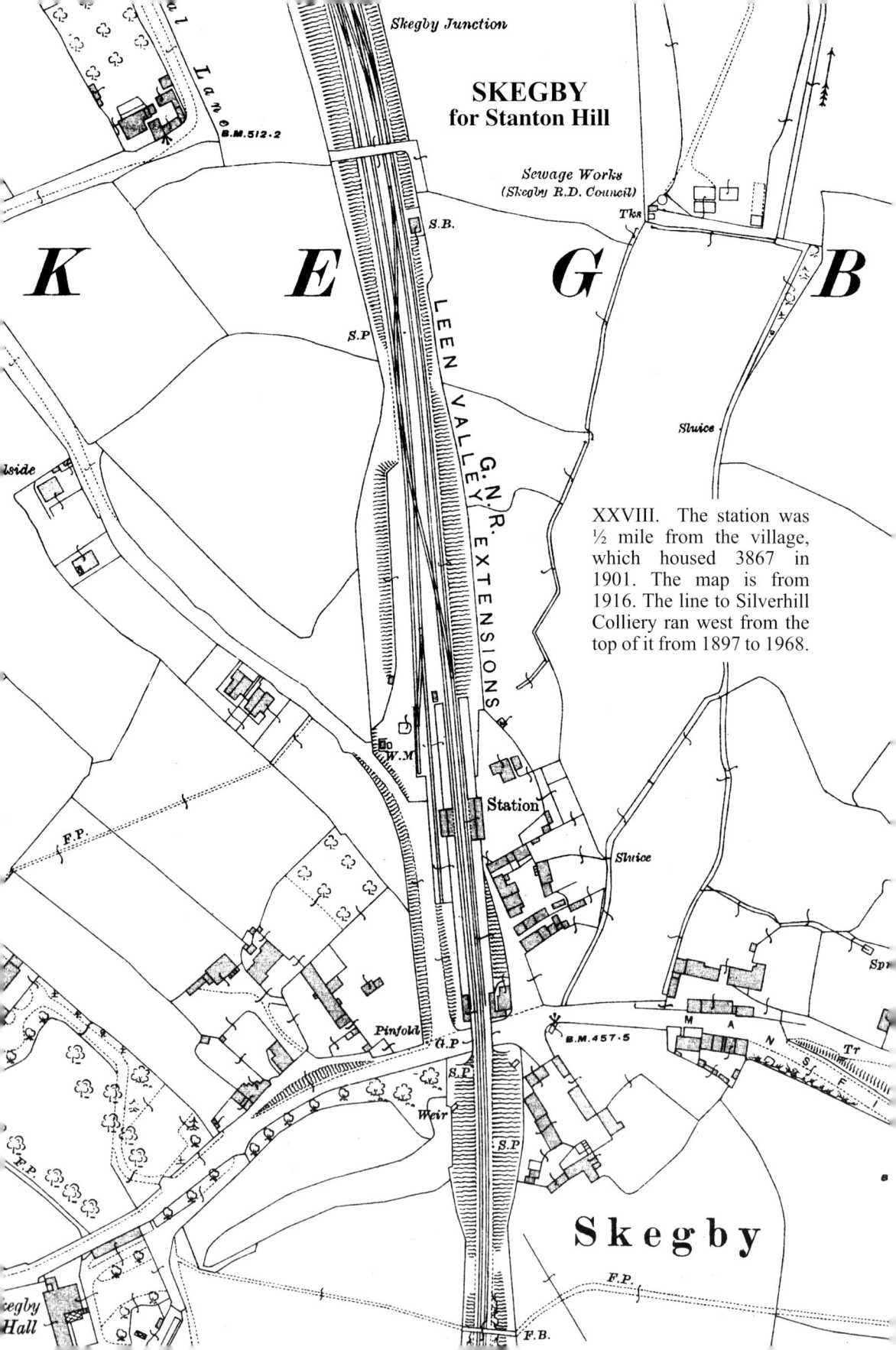

97. The crew of GNR 0-4-4T no. 824 pose in the early era of covered sleepers. The destination in Nottingham is below the number. A regular passenger service was operated from 4th April 1898 until 14th September 1931. (P.Laming coll.)

98. The structures were recorded complete in 1948, but devoid of paperwork and lighting. The wooden platforms have spaced supports. Only two nameboards are evident. (R.Humm coll.)

99. The suffix 'for Stanton Hill' is seen on 2nd July 1955. It first appeared in 1915. Northbound is no. 63751, a class O4 2-8-0, introduced in 1911. Some Summer holiday trains called here on Saturdays from 1954 to 1962. (R.Humm coll.)

100. Working an up goods service on the same day is class 8F 2-8-0 no. 90000, built for use in WWII in 1943. The goods yard had been beyond the building on the left and had closed on 4th August 1952. (R.Humm coll.)

NORTH OF SKEGBY
Skegby Junction

101. A short worker displays his height near a somersault signal arm, above the tiny signal box. Six stay wires are used to stabilise the post. (J.Alsop coll.)

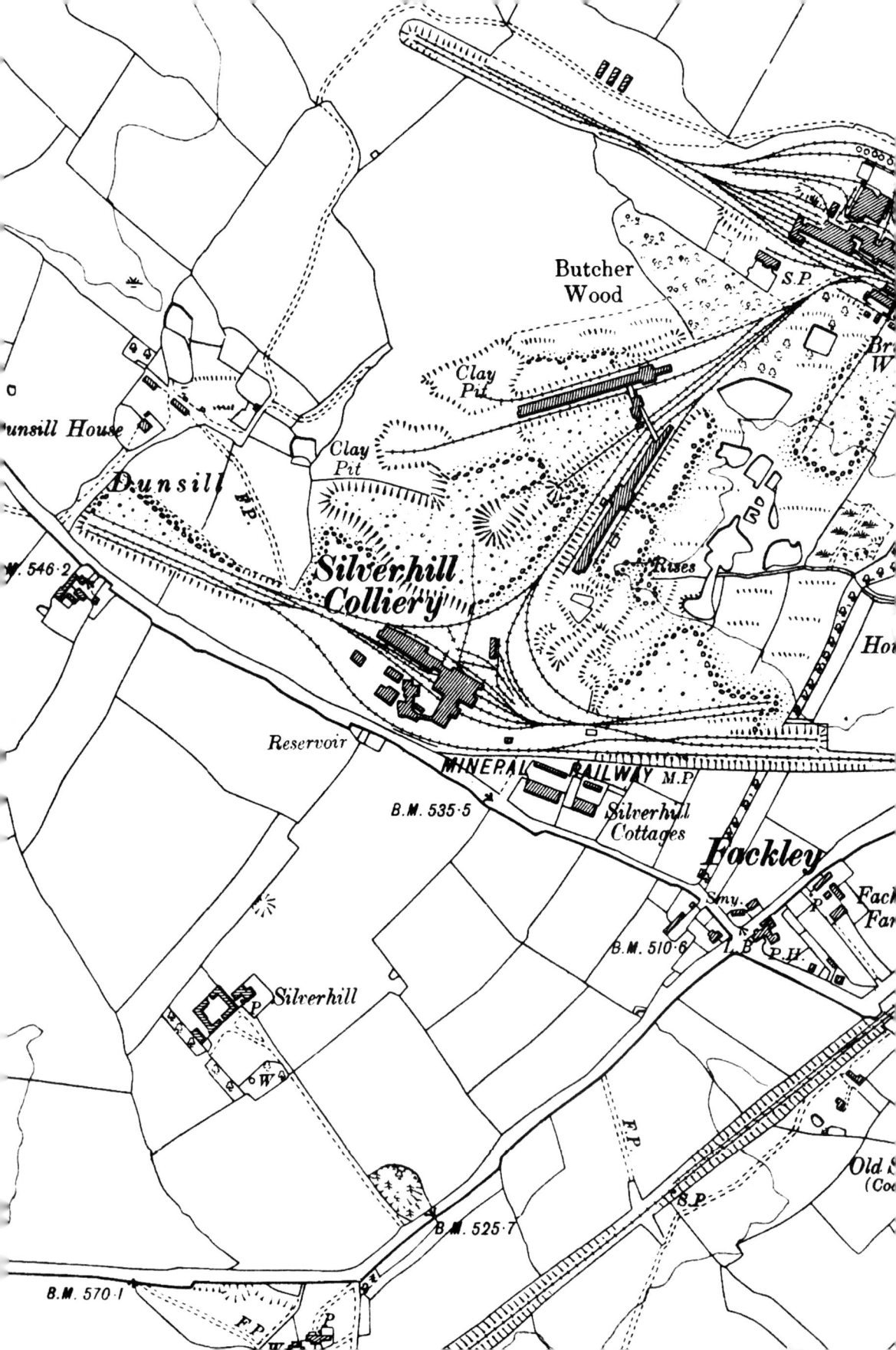

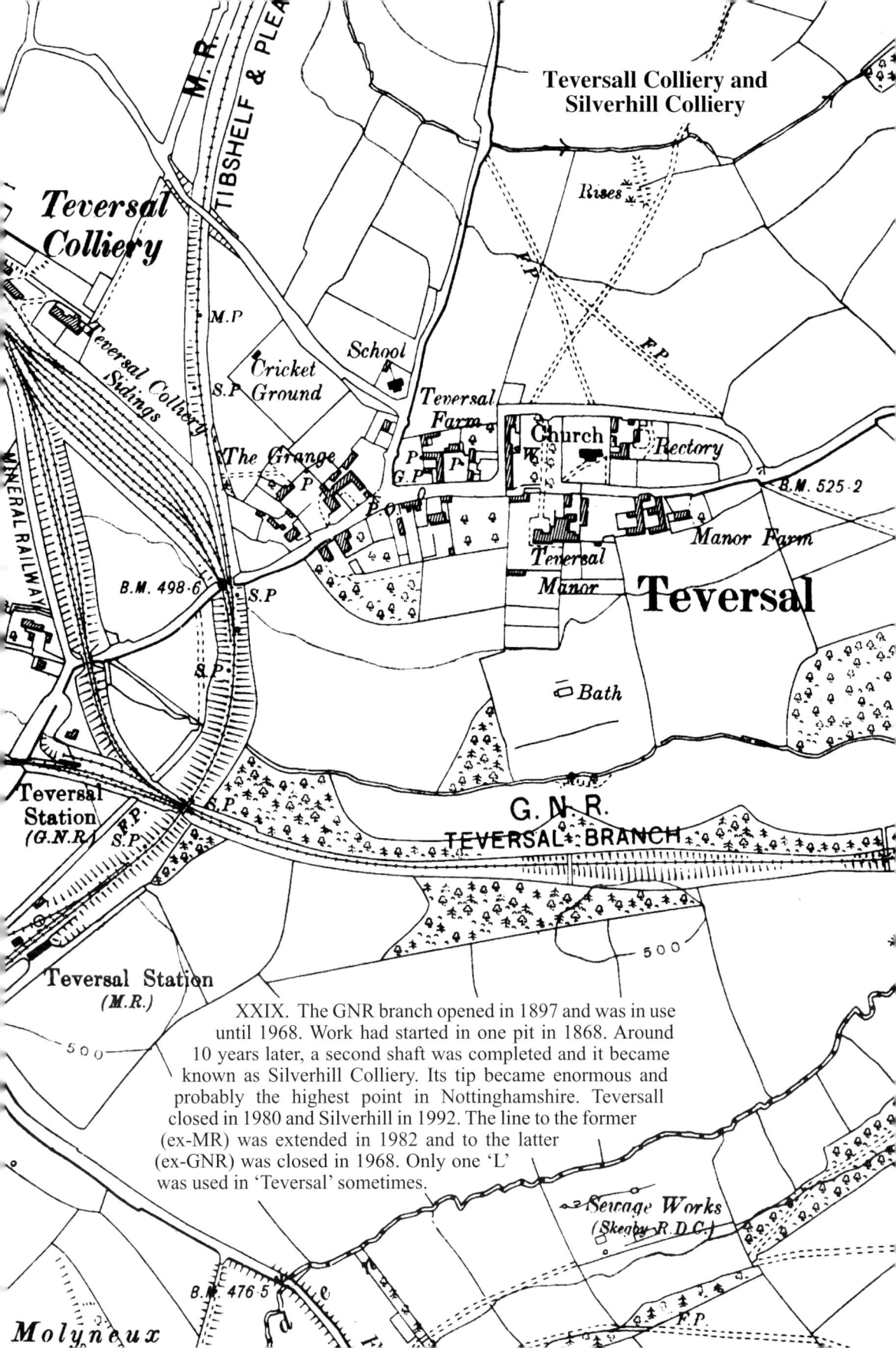

XXIX. The GNR branch opened in 1897 and was in use until 1968. Work had started in one pit in 1868. Around 10 years later, a second shaft was completed and it became known as Silverhill Colliery. Its tip became enormous and probably the highest point in Nottinghamshire. Teversall closed in 1980 and Silverhill in 1992. The line to the former (ex-MR) was extended in 1982 and to the latter (ex-GNR) was closed in 1968. Only one 'L' was used in 'Teversal' sometimes.

102. Map II shows both Teversall stations as closed. We are looking at the ex-GNR one on 19th September 1959, when a railtour was present. It had served the miners only until about 1943, but was later used for excursion traffic, the station name being changed to Teversall East. The MR station was open from 1st May 1886 to 28th July 1930. It was renamed TEVERSALL MANOR for excursion use in 1950-63. (R.Humm coll.)

103. *Churchill*, a standard Barclay 0-6-0ST, was less than three years old when it was photographed shunting at Teversall Colliery on 13th March 1949. The station is on the left border of the right page of the last map. (A.Neale coll.)

Pleasley Colliery Junction

104. We are looking north under the road bridge, which is lower left on the next map. The vista was recorded in about 1920. (J.Alsop coll.)

105. This northward panorama is from 31st March 1967 and was recorded from the centre of the next page. The signal box is shown on it, but not lettered. (R.Humm coll.)

PLEASLEY

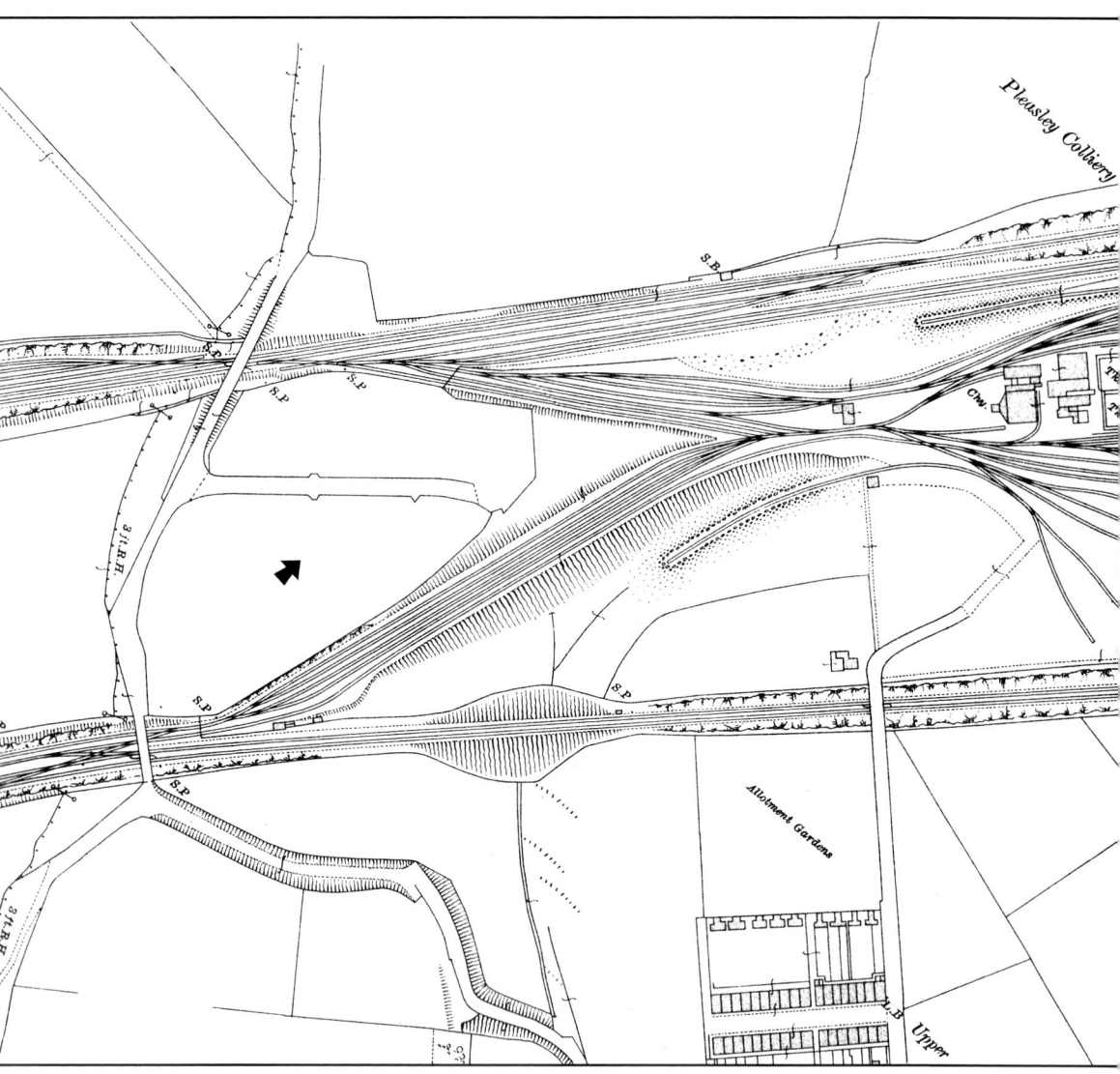

XXX. The ownership of the two routes and stations is shown on this 1916 extract, scaled at about 30ins to 1 mile. They are included left of centre on map II, together with a line running west, termed 'Old Railway'. From 1890 to 1930, it ran north under the A617 to Glapwell Colliery. There were stations called Rowthorn & Hardwick and Glapwell on it. The route through Bolsover northwards was in use from 1884 until 1978.

M.R.
TIBSHELF & PLEASLEY
Station
S.B.
B.M. 445·3
F.P.
S.P.
M.P.
W.M.
Wes. Meth. Chapel
95
6·562
G.N.R.
F.P.
LEEN VALLEY EXTENSIONS
S.Ps
Station
S.B.
Well
Churchstreet Well
CHURCH
Sunday School
Cistern (Covd.)

L. N. E. R.
HALF DAY EXC'N
SKEGNESS
(524) TO
SUTTON-IN-ASHFIELD (Ctral
Valid as per Bills
THIRD
For conditions see back
L. N. E. R.
HALF DAY EXC'N
SUTTON-IN-ASHFIELD Ctral
TO (524)
SKEGNESS
Valid as per Bills
THIRD
For conditions see back
0138
0138

2nd- HOLIDAY PERIOD
Skegness
to
SKEGBY
via Boston & Nottingham
Not available for break of journey
(M) Fare 22/6
For conditions see over
HOLIDAY PERIOD -2nd
Skegby
to
SKEGNESS
via Nottingham & Boston
Not available for break of journey
Fare 22/6 (M)
For conditions see over
0130
0130

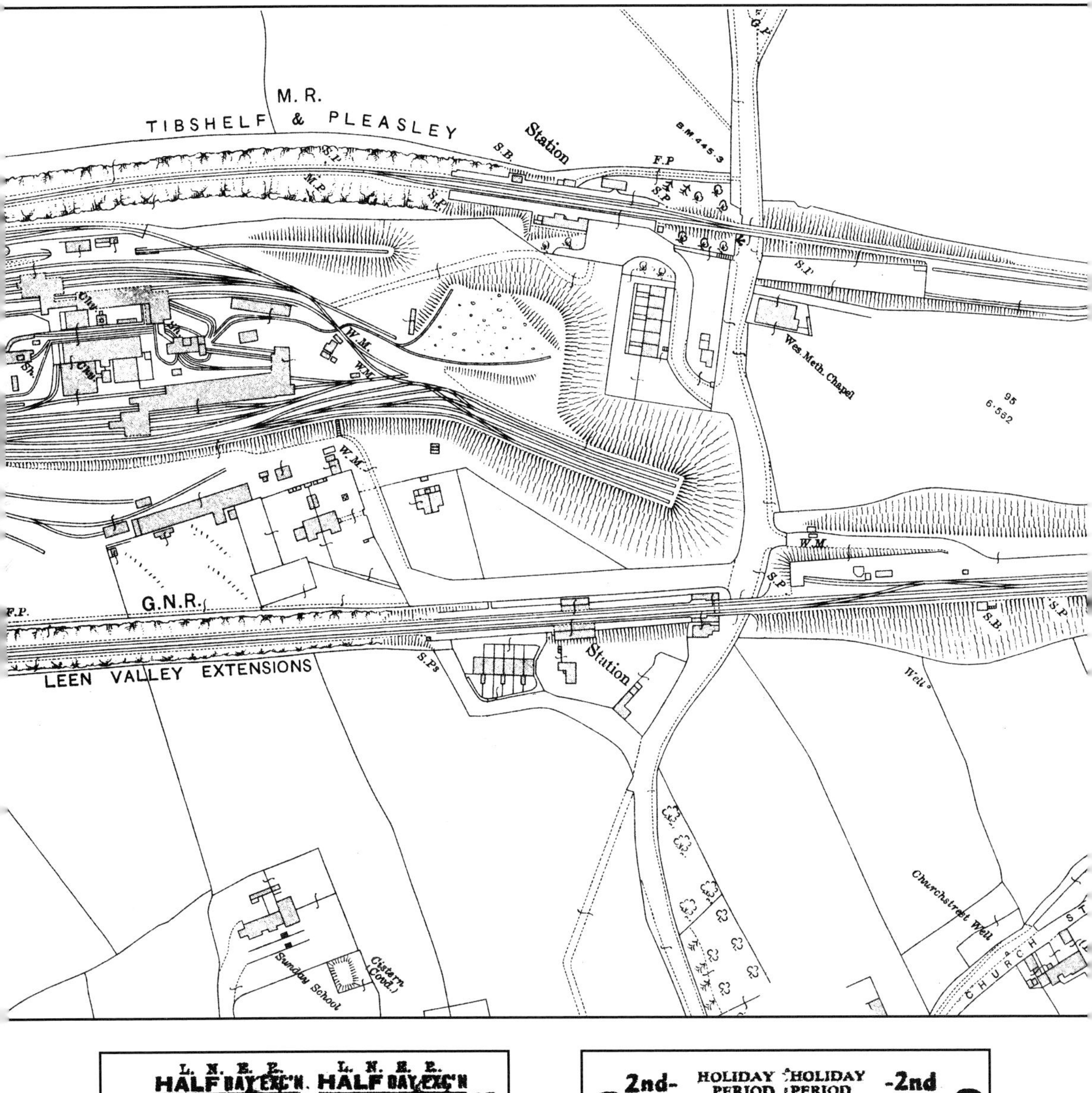

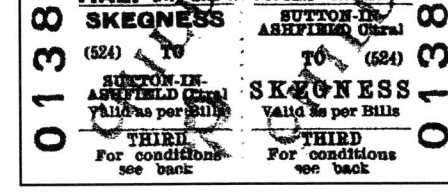

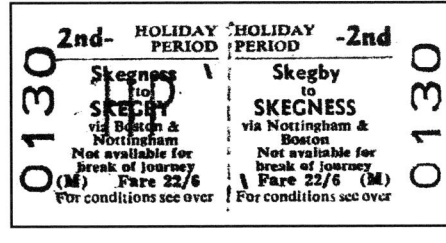

106. This view of the GNR station is looking northeast. Passengers were carried from 1st November 1901 until 14th September 1931. The MR station's dates were 1st May 1886 to 28th July 1930. The goods yard here was beyond the bridge and closed on 7th October 1963; the other one lasted until 1st September 1952. (P.Laming coll.)

Pleasley Colliery

107. Pleasley Colliery was formerly owned by the Stanton Ironworks Company, who purchased many of their locomotives from the Avonside Engine Co at Bristol. No. 5 was an 1895 example and is seen on 31st March 1950. Production started in 1881, when electric lighting was introduced; it was a rare early mine example. Closure came in 1986, but one shaft was used to supply air to Shirebrook. All output was transferred there later. Friends of Pleasley Pit took control of many surface structures and have received heritage awards. (Industrial Railway Society)

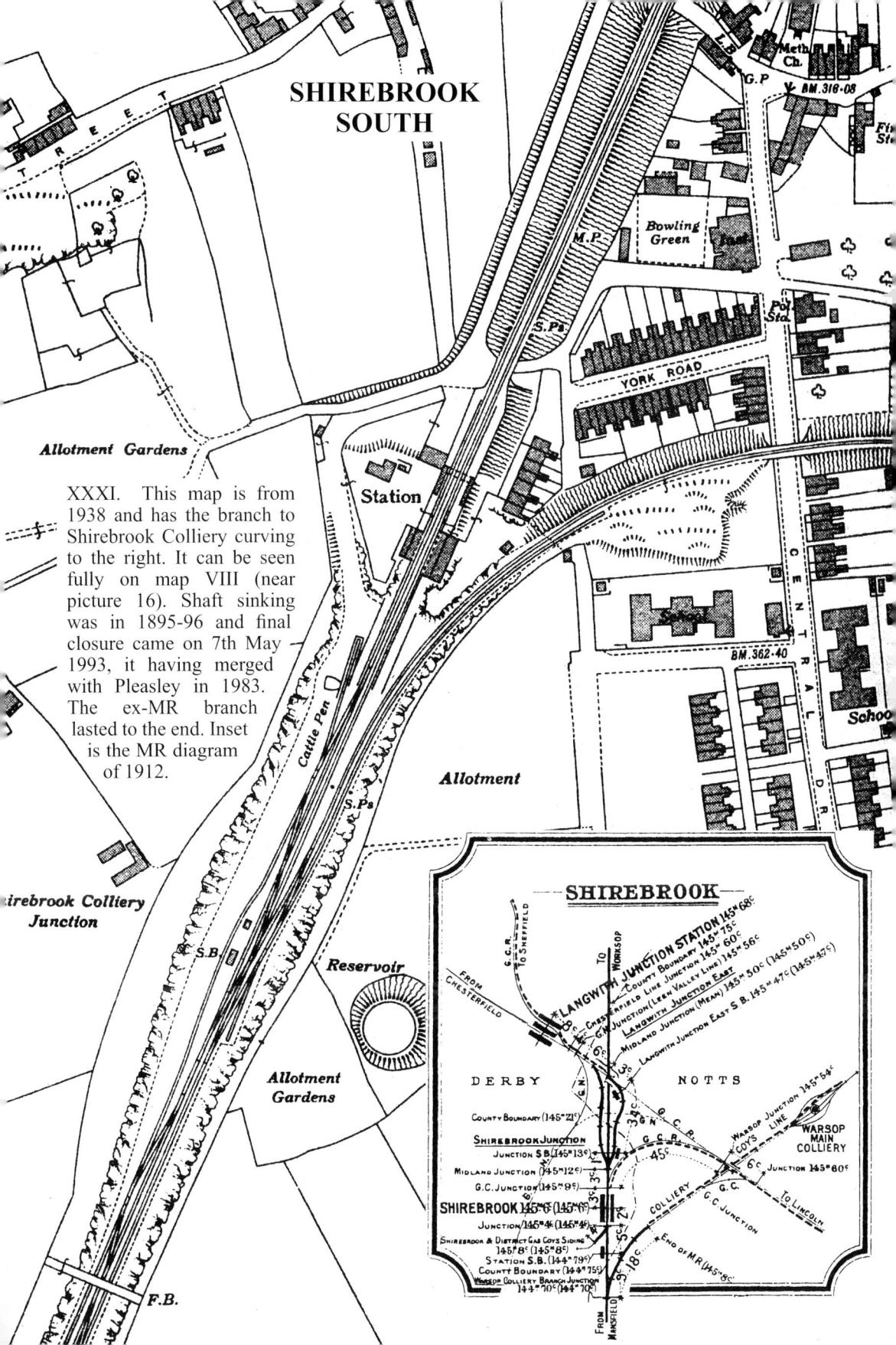

XXXI. This map is from 1938 and has the branch to Shirebrook Colliery curving to the right. It can be seen fully on map VIII (near picture 16). Shaft sinking was in 1895-96 and final closure came on 7th May 1993, it having merged with Pleasley in 1983. The ex-MR branch lasted to the end. Inset is the MR diagram of 1912.

108. A train is southbound in this undated view before the station received the word SOUTH on 2nd June 1924. Regular services ceased on 14th September 1931, but there were a few Summer Saturday trains calling in the 1950s. (J.Alsop coll.)

109. The single signal box is marked S.B. on the map. The goods yard closed on 4th February 1957 and the route saw no trains after 27th May 1968. The map shows a siding in front of and behind the box. It had 40 levers and was in use from 1st January 1899 until 24th May 1959. (J.Alsop coll.)

NORTH OF SHIREBROOK SOUTH

Langwith Junction Engine Shed

110. The sheds are shown near the top of map VIII. They were connected to the GCR, but not to the MR or GNR. The Wagon Works is below them. This was run by a Mr Davis. The coal shed is on the right. The track was raised to reduce the labour of shovelling coal up from wagons into tenders. (J.Alsop coll.)

111. Present on 2nd September 1955 were class J11 0-6-0 no. 64389 and class O4 2-8-0 no. 63679. The coal shed has gone to reveal the locomotive hoist. Code 40E was used in 1950-58 and 41J in 1958-66, when the shed closed. The turntable was beyond the right border. (H.C.Casserley)

112. The coal shed was replaced by the tower on the right. Wagons were hoisted up its right side and tipped into a large bin at the top. In attendance on 19th May 1957 were nos 69929, 90545, 63842, 64427 and 63717. Locos here numbered 81 in 1956. (R.Humm coll.)

LANGWITH JUNCTION

113. There was no access for MR services to this LDECR station until 1904. GNR trains could enter it from 1901. It had four through platforms, with generous canopies, from the outset. The long footbridge is in the background of this eastward view. (P.Laming coll.)

114. Seen from the footbridge, looking east again, is the main tank for locomotive water supply. The two lines on the right are sidings. The bridge carried footpath users, as well as passengers. (R.Humm coll.)

115. The atmosphere of the steam days is well recorded in another footbridge vista. Not one head of hair or an ankle is visible in the crowd in this Edwardian perspective. Four private sidings were listed here for many years between the wars. (P.Laming coll.)

116. The name of the station was changed to Shirebrook North on 2nd June 1924, but the engine shed name remained unaltered. No. 2404 is showing an MR number and a rare tender cab. (R.Humm coll.)

SHIREBROOK NORTH

117. The spacious station is seen on 9th May 1949 as class N5 0-6-2T no. 69327 waits with a Mansfield to Chesterfield service. Again, the great extent of the lattice bridge can be observed. The route west to Bolsover closed fully in 1951. (R.Humm coll.)

118. The 4.20pm from Edwinstowe is terminating here on 4th July 1953. Blowing off is no. 69323, a class N5 0-6-2T, a type dating from 1891 and numbering around 120. The 85-lever box of 1897 was worked until 10th November 1974, when the line north from the station closed. (R.J.Buckley/J.Suter coll.)

119. A suffix eventually appeared on the running-in boards; it was FOR LANGWITH. It was presumably to reduce misunderstandings following the major name change. Closure came for passengers on 19th September 1955 and the goods yard followed on 4th January 1965. (R.Humm coll.)

> **For other views of this station see pictures 17-26 in our** *Chesterfield to Lincoln* **album.**

120. A Summer Saturday service to Skegness continued to call here until 5th September 1964. A staff service ran to Tuxford Depot until 26th August 1961. This view is from 2nd September 1955; the coaches may be full of holiday makers. A simpler footbridge carried the footpath over the one or two lines left from 1960 until 1986. (H.C.Casserley)

MP Middleton Press

EVOLVING THE ULTIMATE RAIL ENCYCLOPEDIA

Easebourne Midhurst GU29 9AZ. Tel:01730 813169

www.middletonpress.co.uk email:info@middletonpress.co.uk
A-978 0 906520 B- 978 1 873793 C- 978 1 901706 D-978 1 904474
E - 978 1 906008 F - 978 1 908174 G - 978 1 910356

Our RAILWAY titles are listed below. Please check availability by looking at our website *middletonpress.co.uk*, telephoning us or by requesting a Brochure which includes our *LATEST* RAILWAY TITLES also our TRAMWAY, TROLLEYBUS, MILITARY and COASTAL series

A
Abergavenny to Merthyr C 91 8
Abertillery & Ebbw Vale Lines D 84 5
Aberystwyth to Carmarthen E 90 1
Allhallows - Branch Line to A 62 8
Alton - Branch Lines to A 11 6
Andover to Southampton A 82 6
Ascot - Branch Lines around A 64 2
Ashburton - Branch Line to B 95 4
Ashford - Steam to Eurostar B 67 1
Ashford to Dover A 48 2
Austrian Narrow Gauge D 04 3
Avonmouth - BL around D 42 5
Aylesbury to Rugby D 91 3

B
Baker Street to Uxbridge D 90 6
Bala to Llandudno E 87 1
Banbury to Birmingham D 27 2
Banbury to Cheltenham E 63 5
Bangor to Holyhead F 01 7
Bangor to Portmadoc E 72 7
Barking to Southend C 80 2
Barmouth to Pwllheli E 53 6
Barry - Branch Lines around D 50 0
Bartlow - Branch Lines to F 27 7
Basingstoke to Salisbury A 89 4
Bath Green Park to Bristol C 36 9
Bath to Evercreech Junction A 60 4
Beamish 40 years on rails E94 9
Bedford to Wellingborough D 31 9
Berwick to Drem F 64 2
Berwick to St. Boswells F 75 8
B'ham to Tamworth & Nuneaton F 63 5
Birkenhead to West Kirby F 61 1
Birmingham to Wolverhampton E253
Blackburn to Hellifield F 95 6
Bletchley to Cambridge D 94 4
Bletchley to Rugby E 07 9
Bodmin - Branch Lines around B 83 1
Boston to Lincoln F 80 2
Bournemouth to Evercreech Jn A 46 8
Bournemouth to Weymouth A 57 4
Bradshaw's History F18 5
Bradshaw's Rail Times 1850 F 13 0
Branch Lines series - see town names
Brecon to Neath D 43 2
Brecon to Newport D 16 6
Brecon to Newtown E 06 2
Brighton to Eastbourne A 16 1
Brighton to Worthing A 03 1
Bristol to Taunton D 03 6
Bromley South to Rochester B 23 7
Bromsgrove to Birmingham D 87 6
Bromsgrove to Gloucester D 73 9
Broxbourne to Cambridge F16 1
Brunel - A railtour D 74 6
Bude - Branch Line to B 29 9
Burnham to Evercreech Jn B 68 0

C
Cambridge to Ely D 55 5
Canterbury - BLs around B 58 9
Cardiff to Dowlais (Cae Harris) E 47 5
Cardiff to Pontypridd E 95 6
Cardiff to Swansea E 42 0
Carlisle to Hawick E 85 7
Carmarthen to Fishguard E 66 6
Caterham & Tattenham Corner B251
Central & Southern Spain NG E 91 8
Chard and Yeovil - BLs a C 30 7
Charing Cross to Dartford A 75 8
Charing Cross to Orpington A 96 3
Cheddar - Branch Line to B 90 9
Cheltenham to Andover C 43 7
Cheltenham to Redditch D 81 4
Chesterfield to Lincoln G 21 0
Chester to Birkenhead F 21 5
Chester to Manchester F 51 2
Chester to Rhyl E 93 2
Chester to Warrington F 40 6
Chichester to Portsmouth A 14 7
Clacton and Walton - BLs to F 04 8
Clapham Jn to Beckenham Jn B 36 7
Cleobury Mortimer - BLs a E 18 5
Clevedon & Portishead - BLs to D180
Consett to South Shields E 57 4
Cornwall Narrow Gauge D 56 2
Corris and Vale of Rheidol E 65 9
Coventry to Leicester G 00 5
Craven Arms to Llandeilo E 35 2
Craven Arms to Wellington E 33 8
Crawley to Littlehampton A 34 5
Crewe to Manchester F 57 4
Crewe to Wigan G 12 8
Cromer - Branch Lines around C 26 0
Croydon to East Grinstead B 48 0
Crystal Palace & Catford Loop B 87 1
Cyprus Narrow Gauge E 13 0

D
Darjeeling Revisited F 09 3
Darlington Leamside Newcastle E 28 4
Darlington to Newcastle D 98 2
Dartford to Sittingbourne B 34 3
Denbigh - Branch Lines around F 32 1
Derby to Chesterfield G 11 1
Derby to Stoke-on-Trent F 93 2
Derwent Valley - BL to the D 06 7
Devon Narrow Gauge E 09 3
Didcot to Banbury D 02 9
Didcot to Swindon C 84 0
Didcot to Winchester C 13 0
Diss to Norwich G 22 7
Dorset & Somerset NG D 76 0
Douglas - Laxey - Ramsey E 75 8
Douglas to Peel C 88 8
Douglas to Port Erin C 55 0
Douglas to Ramsey D 39 5
Dover to Ramsgate A 78 9
Drem to Edinburgh G 06 7
Dublin Northwards in 1950s E 31 4
Dunstable - Branch Lines to E 27 7

E
Ealing to Slough C 42 0
Eastbourne to Hastings A 27 7
East Cornwall Mineral Railways D 22 7
East Croydon to Three Bridges A 53 6
Eastern Spain Narrow Gauge E 56 7
East Grinstead - BLs to A 07 9
East Kent Light Railway A 61 1
East London - Branch Lines of C 44 4
East London Line B 80 0
East of Norwich - Branch Lines E 69 7
Effingham Junction - BLs a A 74 1
Ely to Norwich C 90 1
Enfield Town & Palace Gates D 32 6
Epsom to Horsham A 30 7
Eritrean Narrow Gauge E 38 3
Euston to Harrow & Wealdstone C 89 5
Exeter to Barnstaple B 15 2
Exeter to Newton Abbot C 49 9
Exeter to Tavistock B 69 5
Exmouth - Branch Lines to B 00 8

F
Fairford - Branch Line to A 52 9
Falmouth, Helston & St. Ives C 74 1
Fareham to Salisbury A 67 3
Faversham to Dover B 05 3
Felixstowe & Aldeburgh - BL to D 20 3
Fenchurch Street to Barking C 20 8
Festiniog - 50 yrs of enterprise C 83 3
Festiniog 1946-55 E 01 7
Festiniog in the Fifties B 68 8
Festiniog in the Sixties B 91 6
Ffestiniog in Colour 1955-82 F 25 3
Finsbury Park to Alexandra Pal C 02 8
French Metre Gauge Survivors F 88 8
Frome to Bristol B 77 0

G
Gainsborough to Sheffield G 17 3
Galashiels to Edinburgh F 52 9
Gloucester to Bristol D 35 7
Gloucester to Cardiff D 66 1
Gosport - Branch Lines around A 36 9
Greece Narrow Gauge D 72 2
Guildford to Redhill A 63 5

H
Hampshire Narrow Gauge D 36 4
Harrow to Watford D 14 2
Harwich & Hadleigh - BLs to F 02 4
Harz Revisited F 62 8
Hastings to Ashford A 37 6
Hawick to Galashiels F 36 9
Hawkhurst - Branch Line to A 66 6
Hayling - Branch Line to A 12 3
Hay-on-Wye - BL around D 92 0
Haywards Heath to Seaford A 28 4
Hemel Hempstead - BLs to D 88 3
Henley, Windsor & Marlow - BLa C77 2
Hereford to Newport D 54 8
Hertford & Hatfield - BLs a E 58 1
Hertford Loop E 71 0
Hexham to Carlisle D 75 3
Hexham to Hawick F 08 6
Hitchin to Peterborough D 07 4
Holborn Viaduct to Lewisham A 81 9
Horsham - Branch Lines to A 02 4
Huntingdon - Branch Line to A 93 2

I
Ilford to Shenfield C 97 0
Ilfracombe - Branch Line to B 21 3
Ipswich to Diss F 81 9
Ipswich to Saxmundham C 41 3
Isle of Man Railway Journey F 94 9
Isle of Wight Lines - 50 yrs C 12 3
Italy Narrow Gauge F 17 8

K
Kent Narrow Gauge C 45 1
Kettering to Nottingham F 82-6
Kidderminster to Shrewsbury E 10 9
Kingsbridge - Branch Line to C 98 7
Kings Cross to Potters Bar E 62 8
King's Lynn to Hunstanton F 58 1
Kingston & Hounslow Loops A 83 3
Kingswear - Branch Line to C 17 8

L
Lambourn - Branch Line to C 70 3
Launceston & Princetown - BLs C 19 2
Leek - Branch Line From G 01 2
Leicester to Burton F 85 7
Leicester to Nottingham G 15 9
Lewisham to Dartford A 92 5
Lincoln to Cleethorpes F 56 7
Lincoln to Doncaster G 03 6
Lines around Stamford F 98 7
Lines around Wimbledon B 75 6
Liverpool Street to Chingford D 01 2
Liverpool Street to Ilford C 34 5
Llandeilo to Swansea E 46 8
London Bridge to Addiscombe B 20 6
London Bridge to East Croydon A 58 1
Longmoor - Branch Lines to A 41 3
Looe - Branch Line to C 22 2
Loughborough to Chesterfield G 24 1
Loughborough to Nottingham F 68 0
Lowestoft - BLs around E 40 6
Ludlow to Hereford E 14 7
Lydney - Branch Lines around E 26 0
Lyme Regis - Branch Line to A 45 1
Lynton - Branch Line to B 04 6

M
Machynlleth to Barmouth E 54 3
Maesteg and Tondu Lines F 06 2
Majorca & Corsica Narrow Gauge F 41 3
Mansfield to Doncaster G 23 4
March - Branch Lines around B 09 1
Market Drayton - BLs around F 67 3
Market Harborough to Newark F 86 4
Marylebone to Rickmansworth D 49 4
Melton Constable to Yarmouth Bch E031
Midhurst - Branch Lines of E 78 9
Midhurst - Branch Lines to F 00 0
Minehead - Branch Line to A 80 2
Mitcham Junction Lines B 01 5
Monmouth - Branch Lines to E 20 8
Monmouthshire Eastern Valleys D 71 5
Moretonhampstead - BL to C 27 7
Moreton-in-Marsh to Worcester D 26 5
Morpeth to Bellingham F 87 1
Mountain Ash to Neath D 80 7

N
Newark to Doncaster F 78 9
Newbury to Westbury C 66 6
Newcastle to Hexham D 69 2
Newport (IOW) - Branch Lines to A 26 0
Newquay - Branch Lines to C 71 0
Newton Abbot to Plymouth C 60 4
Newtown to Aberystwyth E 41 3
Northampton to Peterborough F 92 5
North East German NG D 44 9
Northern Alpine Narrow Gauge F 37 6
Northern France Narrow Gauge C 75 8
Northern Spain Narrow Gauge E 83 3
North London Line B 94 7
North of Birmingham F 55 0
North of Grimsby - Branch Lines G 09 8
North Woolwich - BLs around C 65 9
Nottingham to Boston F 70 3
Nottingham to Lincoln F 43 7
Nuneaton to Loughborough G 08 1

O
Ongar - Branch Line to E 05 5
Orpington to Tonbridge B 03 9
Oswestry - Branch Lines around E 60 4
Oswestry to Whitchurch E 81 9
Oxford to Bletchley D 57 9
Oxford to Moreton-in-Marsh D 15 9

P
Paddington to Ealing C 37 6
Paddington to Princes Risborough C819
Padstow - Branch Line to B 54 1
Peebles Loop G 19 7
Pembroke and Cardigan - BLs to F 29 1
Peterborough to Kings Lynn E 32 1
Peterborough to Lincoln F 89 5
Peterborough to Newark F 72 7
Plymouth - BLs around B 98 5
Plymouth to St. Austell C 63 5
Pontypool to Mountain Ash D 65 4
Pontypridd to Merthyr F 14 7
Pontypridd to Port Talbot E 86 4
Porthmadog 1954-94 - BLa B 31 2
Portmadoc 1923-46 - BLa B 13 8
Portsmouth to Southampton A 31 4
Portugal Narrow Gauge E 67 3
Potters Bar to Cambridge D 70 8
Preston to Blackpool G 16 6
Princes Risborough - BL to D 05 0
Princes Risborough to Banbury C 85 7

R
Railways to Victory C 16 1
Reading to Basingstoke B 27 5
Reading to Didcot C 79 6
Reading to Guildford A 47 5
Redhill to Ashford A 73 4
Return to Blaenau 1970-82 C 64 2
Rhyl to Bangor F 15 4
Rhymney & New Tredegar Lines E 48 2
Rickmansworth to Aylesbury D 61 6
Romania & Bulgaria NG E 23 9
Romneyrail C 32 1
Ross-on-Wye - BLs around E 30 7
Ruabon to Barmouth E 84 0
Rugby to Birmingham E 37 6
Rugby to Loughborough F 12 3
Rugby to Stafford F 07 9
Rugeley to Stoke-on-Trent F 90 1
Ryde to Ventnor A 19 2

S
Salisbury to Westbury B 39 8
Salisbury to Yeovil B 06 0
Sardinia and Sicily Narrow Gauge F 50 5
Saxmundham to Yarmouth C 69 7
Saxony & Baltic Germany Revisited F 71 0
Saxony Narrow Gauge D 47 0
Seaton & Sidmouth - BLs to A 95 6
Selsey - Branch Line to A 04 8
Sheerness - Branch Line to B 16 2
Sheffield towards Manchester G 18 0
Shenfield to Ipswich E 96 3
Shrewsbury - Branch Line to A 86 4
Shrewsbury to Chester E 70 3
Shrewsbury to Crewe F 48 2
Shrewsbury to Ludlow E 21 5
Shrewsbury to Newtown E 29 1
Sierra Leone Narrow Gauge D 28 9
Sirhowy Valley Line E 12 3
Sittingbourne to Ramsgate A 90 1
Skegness & Mablethorpe - BL to F 84 0
Slough to Newbury C 56 7
South African Two-foot gauge E 51 2
Southampton to Bournemouth A 42 0
Southend & Southminster BLs E 76 5
Southern Alpine Narrow Gauge F 22 2
Southern France Narrow Gauge C 47 5
South London Line B 46 6
South Lynn to Norwich City F 03 1
Southwold - Branch Line to A 15
Spalding - Branch Lines around E
Spalding to Grimsby F 65 9 6
Stafford to Chester F 34 5
Stafford to Wellington F 59 8
St Albans to Bedford D 08 1
St. Austell to Penzance C 67 3
St. Boswell to Berwick F 44 4
Steaming Through Isle of Wight A
Stourbridge to Wolverhampton E
St. Pancras to Barking D 68 5
St. Pancras to Folkestone E 88 8
St. Pancras to St. Albans C 78 9
Stratford to Cheshunt F 53 6
Stratford-u-Avon to Birmingham D
Stratford-u-Avon to Cheltenham C
Sudbury - Branch Lines to F 19 2
Surrey Narrow Gauge C 87 1
Sussex Narrow Gauge C 68 0
Swaffham - Branch Lines around F
Swanage to 1999 - BL to A 33 8
Swanley to Ashford B 45 9
Swansea - Branch Lines around F
Swansea to Carmarthen E 59 8
Swindon to Bristol C 96 3
Swindon to Gloucester D 46 3
Swindon to Newport D 30 2
Swiss Narrow Gauge C 94 9

T
Talyllyn 60 E 98 7
Tamworth to Derby F 76 5
Taunton to Barnstaple B 60 2
Taunton to Exeter C 82 6
Taunton to Minehead F 39 0
Tavistock to Plymouth B 88 6
Tenterden - Branch Line to A 21 5
Three Bridges to Brighton A 35 2
Tilbury Loop C 86 4
Tiverton - BLs around C 62 8
Tivetshall to Beccles D 41 8
Tonbridge to Hastings A 44 4
Torrington - Branch Lines to B 37
Tourist Railways of France G 04 3
Towcester - BLs around E 39 0
Tunbridge Wells BLs A 32 1

U
Upwell - Branch Line to B 64 0
Uttoxeter to Macclesfield G 05 0

V
Victoria to Bromley South A 98 7
Victoria to East Croydon A 40 6
Vivarais Revisited E 08 6

W
Walsall Routes F 45 1
Wantage - Branch Line to D 25 8
Wareham to Swanage 50 yrs D 09
Waterloo to Windsor A 54 3
Waterloo to Woking A 38 3
Watford to Leighton Buzzard D 45
Wellingborough to Leicester F 73 4
Welshpool to Llanfair E 49 9
Wenford Bridge to Fowey C 09 3
Westbury to Bath B 55 8
Westbury to Taunton C 76 5
West Cornwall Mineral Rlys D 48 7
West Croydon to Epsom B 08 4
West German Narrow Gauge D 93
West London - BLs of C 50 5
West London Line B 84 8
West Wiltshire - BLs of D 12 8
Weymouth - BLs A 65 9
Willesden Jn to Richmond B 71 8
Wimbledon to Beckenham C 58 1
Wimbledon to Epsom B 62 6
Wimborne - BLs around A 97 0
Wirksworth - Branch Lines to G 10
Wisbech - BLs around C 01 7
Witham & Kelvedon - BLs a E 82 6
Woking to Alton A 59 8
Woking to Portsmouth A 25 3
Woking to Southampton A 55 0
Wolverhampton to Shrewsbury E 4
Wolverhampton to Stafford F 79 6
Worcester to Birmingham D 97 5
Worcester to Hereford D 38 8
Worthing to Chichester A 06 2
Wrexham to New Brighton F 47 5
Wroxham - BLs around F 31 4

Y
Yeovil - 50 yrs change C 38 3
Yeovil to Dorchester A 76 5
Yeovil to Exeter A 91 8
York to Scarborough F 23 9